French Style

BY SUZANNE SLESIN
& STAFFORD CLIFF
PHOTOGRAPHS BY JACQUES DIRAND

Preface by Andrée Putman
Foreword by Robert Rosenblum
Design by Stafford Cliff

Consultants
Marie-Claude Dumoulin • Marie-Paule Pellé • Bénédicte Siroux
Research assistant • June Petrie

Thames and Hudson

To the memories of
Jane West, Beno Slesin,
and Ronda Cliff

French Style

First published in Great Britain in 1982
by Thames and Hudson Ltd, London

French Style has been an international endeavor, with a year of transatlantic peregrinations and telephone calls. It would never have been finished, or even started, were it not for the help of writers, designers, and friends who relayed information and mail across the Atlantic.

Our thanks:
to all the people who allowed their homes to be photographed and included;
to the editors, writers, and stylists who originally discovered many of the places that appear in this book and who set the highest standards for us to emulate. Their articles provided us with information without which French Style *could not have been written. We are especially grateful to Marie-Claude Dumoulin of* Elle, *our collaborator and a most talented scout, writer, and editor; Jean-Charles Dedieu, Jacques Garai, and Pompon Bailhache of* Marie Claire; *Marielle Hucliez, Daniel Lattes, Marie-Paule Pellé, and Claire Hirsch-Marie, of* Maison de Marie Claire; *Paule Verchère, Misha de Podestad, and Jacqueline Demornex of* Elle; *Jean-Pierre Marche, Caroline Lebeau, and Pamela Dieu of* 100 Idées, *and Jean-Louis Gaillemin of* Architectural Digest. *Their articles enabled us to understand the photographs of homes we were not able to visit firsthand;*

ACKNOWLEDGMENTS

to the Service SCOOP of Elle and the magazine Architektur und Wohnen, and Charles Ross and Penny Glassell of Architectural Digest, who were particularly efficient and granted us special permission to use the photographs of the château decorated by Dick Dumas, which can be seen on pages 160 through 163. The photographs were originally published in Architectural Digest in July/August 1980;

to many of our friends and colleagues, who provided us with invaluable clues, historical information, and personal recollections when it came to trying to define the French style. Our thanks especially to Andrée Putman and Robert Rosenblum, who wrote the preface and the foreword; and to Francois Baudot, Jean-Paul Beaujard, Marc Berthier, Gilles de Bure, John Loring, Rita Reif, and Daniel Rozensztroch, who provided information for the writing of the text;

to Leyland Gomez in London and Thomas Bodkin in New York for their typographic expertise, advice, and assistance; Ian Hammond, who drew up all the transparencies and handled the production; Graham Boad, who produced many high quality color prints, and Andrew Petit, who printed the grid sheets; Alex McLean, assistant to Jacques Dirand, who was a tireless translator; Wendy Sclight, who provided editing advice; and Niels Kummer, who translated a German magazine article we needed in a hurry;

to the many others in England, France, and the United States, who enthusiastically gave us with locations and sources, advice and continued support. They include: Mattia Bonetti, David Brittain, Jacqueline Dufour and her sister Frédérique Baligan, Dona Guimaraes, Serge Korniloff, Mary Smith, and Barbara Isenberg, Murielle and Lionel Labrousse, Hitch Lyman, Eric Philippe, Bernard and Laura Ruiz-Picasso, Mort Stone, Christopher Wilk, Sharon Zane, Michèle and Gilles Mahé, Monique Petit, Jean and Dorothée d'Orgeval, Michèle Chauvel, and Jacques Grange. Each made a special contribution and helped us get this book done on time;

to Bénédicte Siroux, who organized much of the material, located invaluable sources, and tenaciously followed through until photographs and permissions were in hand; and June Petrie who was an efficient coordinator of all the disparate pieces that make up this book, and who prepared the dossier;

to Robert Levin, who photographed the products for the dossier with the assistance of David Kelley; and the department stores, retailers, and manufacturers who cooperated with us on its preparation by sending in catalogs and lending us merchandise for photography;

to the many who provided extra assistance: Arlene Hirst of the Pottery Barn; Duane Garrison of Tiffany & Company; Gregory Turpan and David Sanders of Turpan Sanders; Phil Fligstein of Terraillon; Barry Harwood of Harwood Galleries; Michel Fortin; Jeanette, Amy, and Elizabeth Gavaris of Jenny B. Goode; Judith Auchincloss and Julia MacFarlane of Manhattan Ad Hoc Housewares; William Schoenfisch; Richard Falcone of Cafco; Howard Kaplan of the French Country Store; Barbara Orbach of Cherchez; Margo Rogoff of Bloomingdale's; Susan Freedman of Clarence House; Judy Cohen of Macy's; Alan Moss; and Primrose Bordier and Marie Turolla of Descamps;

to Terence Conran for his enthusiasm about this project and for the inspiration that The House Book provided; to Maria Kroll, for her guidance and encouragement when this book was but an idea; to John Stephenson, managing director of Conran Associates, for his support; and to our agent Lucy Kroll, who believed in French Style from the time she saw the first photograph;

to Jane West, the late publisher of Clarkson N. Potter, Inc., who did not see the completion of this book but gave it impetus and direction from its beginnings;

to Carol Southern and Michael Fragnito of Clarkson N. Potter, Inc., and especially to Teresa Nicholas, as well as Ann Cahn, Lynne Arany, Ellen Tarlow, George Oehl, and Alice Sachs, all of whom extended themselves for us beyond the normal limits of their jobs;

to our editor Nancy Novogrod to whom we owe a special debt. Through weeks and weekends she tirelessly monitored and made suggestions as to the copy and content of French Style. The attention and sound advice she brought to the project are apparent. If there is clumsiness or ambiguity, that is our responsibility, not hers.

Finally, to those who for months lived in international time zones—Michael Steinberg, a patient editorial adviser, simultaneous translator, and headline writer; John Scott, expert messagetaker and organizer who never lost his patience, even under really extenuating circumstances; and Yveline Hollier-Larousse, who was a helpful interpreter and peacemaker.

Suzanne Slesin, New York
Stafford Cliff, London
Jacques Dirand, Paris
December 1981

The antique cupboard in Monique Petit's turn-of-the-century Paris house holds china for use in the dining room.

CONTENTS

PREFACE

ANDRÉE PUTMAN

is a Paris-based designer. Her company, Ecart
International, produces furniture designed by architects in
the 1920s and 1930s.

"His giant wings prevent him from flying."
Charles Baudelaire, "L'Albatros"

Having been born into what it is convenient to call the
cradle of good taste, I felt very early on a desire to fight
against that old French conception of the ideal, which
seemed much like a teddy bear worn out by affection.
Classic French style, caught in the trap of its own
history, stumbles over tassels, sneezes among velvets
and brocades, dozes in fake Louis XV armchairs, and is
suffocated by its overly rich past: "Trianon" blue, "Empire" green, obsessively period rooms, and, worse, the
re-creation of styles that were already tiresome in their

time. One sees sinister domed bronze clocks exactly centered on mantels with, at their most horrible, candlesticks left and right. Worse still, the candles are never lit. Yes, one is quickly bored to death, and quickly driven to extremism. Too often Versailles lights up the hearts of the French. The spirit of Narcissus strolling the Hall of Mirrors has wreaked havoc. I find I have a score to settle with this renowned French taste.

Happily, one more and more frequently comes upon houses that are alive and free; homes that describe their inhabitants. Respectability and concern over sound investments have been abandoned in favor of charm, spontaneity, and eclecticism. This tendency toward the casual is nothing other than elegance, and this too, happily, one discovers more and more.

It is through an impassioned choice of furniture, objects, and spaces, and through the luxury of the unexpected that houses sometimes are sublime. Thus, to decide how and with what we live, where we dine, where we sleep; to invest enough love in these choices is "to invent." These are where the currents of the life we lead flow, and where our personal preferences place their punctuation marks.

We must slowly savor our culture. Swallowed whole it becomes poisonous, a rich draft that turns people into idiots paralyzed by respect. If we learn to discriminate, to choose rather than merely accept, French taste and style can become remarkably fascinating. And as the proverb states, "the best soups are made in old pots." We will no longer be bound by old rules that don't work, but we will not have lost the flavor of our tastes.

It is rare in France to begin at zero; we know nothing of the blank page or of the musical staff without notes. There is always an aunt, godmother, or grandfather to leave us a dresser or a table service. And if not, there are flea markets from which we can invent a past.

These old bits and pieces, which we tolerate in a kind of love/hate relationship, make a very good "fond de sauce." We throw nothing away, and our attics are no longer dumping grounds. One of the first shocks for French people arriving in the United States are those abandoned pieces of furniture one stumbles across in the streets, and which are sometimes great finds. On French sidewalks, one simply never sees such things.

"A certain idea of France," that beautiful, nationalistic expression of Charles de Gaulle, has, alas, somewhat contributed to the burial of first-class taste. Whereas, sometimes, an Anglo-Saxon nonchalance seems to be the key to the success of a home.

I will always remember a Sunday visit to Connecticut. The address indicated the church square of the town, but it was *in* the church that this great lady I had come to see was camping. I entered and discovered a huge "living room," with silk parachutes forming a ceiling "to hide the somewhat excessive height of the steeple." An unforgettable improvisation where a practical solution became poetry.

Only a kind of freedom allows an effective mixture of rich and poor: the lady who wears Saint-Laurent clothing with jewelry from a five-and-dime; the adventuress who uses haute couture fabrics to upholster her chairs; or the mad woman who sets her table with a mixture of sterling silver, antique lace, and paper doilies. We are moving away from the style of "Sunday finest" toward more courageous contrasts. The most precious golden and silver boxes imitate the most modest woven straw baskets. Elegance sometimes derives from this false modesty, from this sophisticated trompe l'oeil, from this insolent pirouette. When everything is too beautiful, we see only what it costs. So what? There is no talent in that. As my father said when leaving an overly done house: "Lots of taste and all bad."

FOREWORD

ROBERT ROSENBLUM
is a Professor of Fine Arts at New York University
and author of many books and articles
on 19th- and 20th-century art.

In a throwaway quip in his magisterial history of 19th- and 20th-century architecture, Henry-Russell Hitchcock referred to the stripped classicism of Auguste Perret's official Paris buildings of the 1930s as defining a *Style Louis XX*. With this, he pinpointed that special French quality we may love or hate, but can instantly recognize—a stubborn clinging to native traditions of elegance, order, and measure even while paying lip service to a clean-slate modernism that would annihilate the historical past.

I still remember vividly my own surprise and half disappointment when I first visited Paris in 1950, a city I had fantasized as so avant-garde that it would make the world of MOMA look like a provincial shadow. But no, Paris, not to mention Lyons or Marseilles, felt as much like the remote past as Venice, and detective work was necessary to track down the visual revolutions of the 20th century that seemed so conspicuous in the States or, in fact, almost anywhere in Western Europe from Copenhagen and Amsterdam to Zurich and Rome. Even the buildings by Le Corbusier, which were so hard to locate in the suburban periphery of Paris, ended up looking like lonely, displaced persons, just as the Knoll furniture store on the Left Bank looked as alien to the French in its aggressive modernity as the airline office of a foreign country. Again and again, building facades echoed the gravity-bound axial lucidity of Beaux Arts designs and reached their mansarded attic heights with the most gentle, reasonable concession to the sky above and to adjacent silhouettes. As for the interiors, rich or poor, "grandes" or "petites," they seemed reflections of Versailles-type ancestors, with wall planes and furniture eternally skewered on symmetrical axes, their subtle geometries and mirrorlike patterns as orderly and inevitable as their ceremonial sequences of rooms. I found them like the structure of those three-course lunches that interrupted one's 20th-century tempo and informality with an old-fashioned A-B-A form. Any heroic gesture from the Brave New World of international design was instantly rendered bizarre and insignificant by the sheer quantity and authority of its older French neighbors. Any changes in life-style seemed no less

doomed. The weight of the past on the present and the future was overwhelming.

Even on the sea, the *Style Louis XX* conquered. Nothing could match the late and lamented S.S. *France*, the precious time capsule that perpetuated the hierarchies and luxuries of the most venerable French traditions, from the display of glamorous people on grand stairways that harked back to those at the Paris Opéra or Versailles to the intricate formal arrangements of glassware, silver, and china. What a leap in style it was from this floating château to the QE2's airport-lounge informality of the swinging 60s! Or take the terrestrial equivalent of the S.S. *France*, Le Mistral, that luxurious French triumph of Trans-European Express trains, which offers on wheels speeding to the Côte d'Azur the late-20th-century equivalent of Le Train Bleu, a veritable Petit Trianon of cut flowers, boutiques, hairdressers, and white table linen, where a liqueur after lunch or dinner feels not like an anachronistic joke on a train but rather a necessity for maintaining the inherited ritual order of French life. And even the Métro, whose praises the likes of Apollinaire and Cendrars sang in the early 20th century for its cubo-futurist modernity in obliterating the civilization embalmed at the Louvre, now makes one's jaw drop with its literally arty efforts to permeate its depths with traditional high culture. The Louvre stop itself now aspires to the cultural heights aboveground; it displays 3-D facsimiles of the museum's sculptural treasures—Egyptian, Greek, or Gothic—all placed in recessed, softly lit niches that create a subway-platform décor that would not be out of place in a Guerlain showroom. And moving west along the same line, from Vincennes to Neuilly, the refugee from the New York subways is startled along the stops of the Champs-Elysées by what again seems an almost dumbfoundingly surrealist mixture of worlds in collision, here stained-glass facsimiles of masterpieces of modern French painting, from Manet to Matisse. What might be flagrant kitsch or madness elsewhere somehow seems to work in Paris, where this traditional respect for art and history is steeped in the very fabric of the city's visual life.

The power of these traditions is so great that to everybody's continuing surprise even the most alarming, dissonant invasions of 20th-century style get quickly swallowed up by the resonant past. Beaubourg itself, despite its Anglo-Italian parentage, was amazingly and speedily Gallicized, as if it were now impossible to feel the living pulse of Paris without it. Its high-tech fantasy of a see-through, dynamic industrial labyrinth recalls not only Les Halles, those vast cathedrals of 19th-century iron and glass, which it replaced to loud protests, but, more up to date, Fernand Léger's wildest oil-on-canvas dreams of a post–World War I blueprint, in spray-paint kindergarten colors, for an immaculate machine aesthetic utopia serving the teeming demands of a new populist culture. And still more, it functions in everyday terms as the most recent heir to those earlier nuclei of Parisian urban life, the Opéra and Saint-Germain-des-Prés, around which cafés, boutiques, book-stores, and tourists could cluster. Beaubourg, it now seems, was always there, part of the French patrimony, and not a foreign body. Even the Tour Montparnasse, that nonstop high-rise skyscraper with its inevitable panoramic restaurant, first brutally ruptured the city's modulated, ground-hugging skyline as if it belonged more to the highway silhouette around downtown Dallas than to southern Paris, but then was gradually absorbed by the past, so that today it seems almost to conduct a symmetrically balanced dialogue about Parisian architecture and history with its once equally shocking ancestor, the Tour Eiffel.

How long will the endangered species of French style and civilization survive? We may feel as confident of their longevity as we may be of the fact that Fiats and Vespas will never penetrate Venice, but what about all those science-fiction communities that have been banished to La Défense, looming high on the distant Parisian horizon like a mirage from *Star Wars?* For just beyond the peripheries of the city is an outer-space zone where strange new buildings, streets, shopfronts, and floating walkways from a future century look as if they were lying in wait for the inevitable day when they will attack head on the old inner city. But when they do, will they mark the end of a long and glorious dynasty, or will they be miraculously transformed into the *Style Louis XXI?*

Right: *The Centre Georges Pompidou, with its high-tech architecture, rises above the buildings of Paris of the past.*

12

INTRODUCTION

"Style is the man himself," noted Georges Louis Leclerc de Buffon, upon his election to the French Academy. Although the 18th-century scientist referred to the way he expressed his ideas on natural history, his comment reflected a typically French attitude in a wider sense, a concern not only with personal expression but also in the concerns of daily life. That sense of style is a primary and pervasive French characteristic.

It also, perhaps, underlies every foreigner's perception of the French. Even the German philosopher Friedrich Nietzsche, in 1888, declared: "I believe only in French culture, and regard everything else in Europe which calls itself 'culture' as a misunderstanding." It is a comment that confirms a uniquely French ability—to be perceived as a more cultured, more elegant, more stylish people, and to make others feel at some disadvantage in not being born French themselves.

For decades, outsiders have had a distinct and sentimental impression of French style as it is illustrated in French interiors. Because an invitation to a French home is proverbially hard to come by, this image is a mirror of literary and historic accounts, visions that are both myth and reality—sympathetically cluttered or starkly empty rooms, which seem always to be warmly lighted and full of ambiance, with a carefully haphazard placement of furniture, well-patinaed walls, silver glistening on the sideboard, and lace neatly hung at the windows.

Specific images spring to mind: the sedate but strikingly composed interiors of Degas' portraits; Vuillard's and Bonnard's intimate and richly evocative domestic scenes; the vibrant south of France window views by Matisse and Picasso—in which the view through the window itself and the way the scene is framed by the room are essential to the composition.

And, unfailingly, there is a special quality of light, iridescent and poetic, that contributes to the sensuousness of well-crafted materials, to the rigorous sense of proportion and order.

In the France re-created by artists, the exterior and interior of the house are intimately joined, held in a very special relationship. And, in reality, the furniture in many French gardens is set up as if in a formal living room. In city apartments and houses, large windows open onto a park, and plants in window boxes are as well nurtured as city trees.

The importance of the French countryside was celebrated by such 19th-century painters as Monet, Corot, and Pissarro, and by such early 20th-century photographers as Eugène Atget. "He wanted to record everything, everywhere, that spoke for a certain notion of France as an ancient civilization in which landscape, architecture and people lived together in total harmony," John Russell, the art critic, wrote of Atget in the *New York Times*.

These artists' images still remain as representations of the France we like to remember. Past and present are interchangeable. The poetic countryside, the simple Parisian street scene, the rhythmic tree-lined boulevard, the lovely half-open window, are all frozen in time, yet we still very much want to believe in their existence.

Foreigners are beginning to admire and appreciate the simplicity of these images. However, alongside this gentle and romantic perception of France, there has always been the fascination with an earlier and grander style, one that has also been inexorably linked to the image of France. This is the style of its kings and emperors, from Louis XV to the Second Empire.

François Baudot, a Parisian designer, has described the period: "While until the end of the 18th century, the world was satisfied in existing, it would from that time forward worry about how it appeared."

The styles of this period have endured, particularly in the United States, where their gaudy reincarnations can be seen in countless Versailles ballrooms, Trianon suites and Fragonard coffee shops—the *Louis l'Hotel Style* that parodies a glorious past. It is reborn in the American French Provincial Style, with its carved gilt and inlaid woodwork, damask upholstery, and flounced draperies, a style no longer reserved for royalty, which has, not inappropriately, found its most ardent admirers in today's middle classes. Not inappropriately, because

a guiding force behind the style's creation was Madame de Pompadour, Louis XV's favorite mistress. "She was the triumph of middle-class taste," said John Loring, design director and vice-president of Tiffany & Company, who suggests that Madame de Pompadour was instrumental in changing the course of the decorative arts in France and throughout Europe. "She was a major force in establishing the porcelain industry in France; she showed them that a teacup can be a very grand affair," added Mr. Loring. "She was the first design director in history."

"It was a *gout de cocotte*," Loring admitted, "but I don't think there is a house in America in which you could not help but identify her taste."

It was the rise of the new bourgeoisie in late-19th-century France that coincided with a pride in the single urban or rural family home, and its complete accouterment that provided a symbol of solidity and security, which is still recalled with pride.

"We had all the comforts," remembers Marc Berthier, a Parisian architect and designer. One of eleven children, he spent most of his childhood at his family's house in Burgundy. "There was a pond stocked with fish, a vegetable garden, and a fruit orchard to feed the household," Berthier explains. "The house was not huge and we were not considered rich, but we had all we needed—iceboxes and fans, basements for wine, attics for furniture, a laundry room and offices. Houses had to be well organized and, most important, independent."

Each room in such houses had its proper furnishings, furnishings that were not interchangeable—the formal sitting room, the large dining room, the kitchen where the head of the household rarely entered.

The traditional aspects of the day-to-day activities of these homes have remained important in the function of the modern French household. Although the bedroom has remained a private and separate domain, it is only recently that the living room has become a place in which to relax.

In the same way that France's contemporary mores are a combination of past traditions and updated views, some of the best and most livable of French interiors represent a similar synthesis. Furthermore, since the beginning of this century, France has been a cultural catalyst, not only receptive to but also nourishing many foreign influences. A variety of furniture designs have been so closely associated with French interiors that one tends to forget that their origins lie elsewhere.

The Thonet bentwood café chair, for example, was first developed and manufactured in Austria at the end of the 19th century. Today, the chairs designed by the Scottish architect Charles Rennie Mackintosh, English Liberty print fabrics, and American antique patchwork quilts are popular throughout France, as are the furniture designs of the Viennese architect Josef Hoffmann, one of the leaders of the Wiener Werkstätte movement, and the work of Eileen Gray, the Irish-born designer and architect whose furniture, of the 1920s and 1930s, is enjoying a revival.

The popularity of the early 20th-century period is still growing—with the recognition that the 1925 Arts Décoratifs exhibition in Paris was one of the most influential design shows of the century. The glass and ceramics pieces represented both a link to the ornate designs of the Art Nouveau style and a step toward the geometric patterns and new ideas of the Art Deco style. While Americans soon embraced the Art Deco style with open arms, Europeans were more cautious at first.

And today, it is the modern rooms of the 1920s, 1930s, and 1940s that are favored among the more avant-garde. With their high ceilings, crisp moldings, and square overscale furniture, as shown in the interiors of Robert Mallet-Stevens and in the work of Jean-Michel Frank, the French designer of the 1920s and 1930s, who brought a sense of drama, a deft use of materials, and refined elegance to the craft of interior decoration, these interiors are more *au courant* than the slick, hard-edged designs that appeared in France with the rise of Italian design in the 1960s.

In terms more of life-style than decor, one of the major influences from abroad is from the United States—with the development of the kitchen as a major focus of the home. Since the 1950s, like children with faces pressed up to the toy shop window, the French have admired the glistening, efficient American kitchens with their compact built-in cabinets and sleek central work islands.

They have installed their versions of such kitchens, sometimes in the former reception rooms of the house. But the more picturesque elements that we readily associate with French kitchens—the black-and-white checkered floor, the neat rows of preserves, the well-worn pine table—are still to be found and belong to the timeless legacy of the rustic country kitchen.

Americans, though, aware of the French concern for gourmet food, tend to be surprised by the simplicity of most French kitchens and charmed by the age and authenticity of century-old furniture and fixtures, which even an overly done renovation, such as the painter Claude Monet's extraordinary blue, white, and yellow kitchen at Giverny, cannot diminish.

In recent years, the notion of regionalism has once again come into fashion, along with a growing appreciation of traditional, everyday native objects—the handsome rustic pottery, the chiaroscuro designs of the Jacquard Français linens, the flower-patterned hand-printed fabrics, the classic copper cookware.

For some it is a celebration of local crafts; for others, it is a sort of adventurous tourism at home. And, because of its varied geography and climates, France has a marvelous diversity of local styles. The tiled roofs of Provence, the stone-walled houses of Brittany, the châteaus of the Loire Valley, the Romanesque cathedrals of the Southwest, all illustrate varied ways of living in harmony with the land—a concept that is deeply entrenched in the French mentality.

Recently, there has been a renewed interest in the preservation and restoration of large houses and an appreciation of the role they played in French life. Those, who can afford to, inject *un coup de jeune* into the high-ceilinged rooms of the 18th and 19th centuries. Paneling is stripped, parquet floors are bleached, formal furniture is loosely slipcovered in canvas or upholstered in men's gray flannel suiting fabric.

When the French accept that classic rooms are a part of a past that cannot be revived, they don't bother trying to reproduce them; instead, they tend to hold onto the more abstract traditional values of the home, which can be exemplified in a diversity of styles that go beyond the stereotypes of bistro chairs and marble-topped tables, of etched glass and Art Nouveau lighting.

But as living spaces change and people find themselves coping with smaller apartments, the solutions and ideas provided by architects and interior designers have created a new kind of sensibility. There is no longer a single style that is unerringly right. While some members of the new generation of designers have chosen to go back in time, others have turned toward a modern style that they can understand, in that it reinterprets and recycles elements from the past.

The lesson the French have learned most readily from visits abroad is that they can change the way they plan the layout of their homes. The recycling of commercial buildings, warehouses, and factories introduced them to the loft, as decades ago the car introduced them to the freedom of escaping for *le weekend*.

"They travel for business in China, Germany, Hungary, and Argentina; they spend their vacations in Greece, Senegal, Bali, and Mexico. They furnish their homes with English pine, Chinese bamboo, Italian design, and Japanese technology," Gilles de Bure, a French journalist and design consultant, observes about his countrymen. "Nothing is less chauvinistic than such habits," adds de Bure. "But the Frenchman, before being French, is Breton or Corsican, Auvergnat or Normand, Basque or Catalan. So nothing is less nationalistic than such attitudes."

This may be the reason that the French are embracing the high-tech style energetically, if not wholeheartedly, remaining more timid in terms of the hardier interpretations of the industrial style. Even when converting a raw commerical space, they infused their lofts with a sense of restraint and refinement, keeping the large open spaces always under control, often by creating more traditional room layouts, or opting for a vertical arrangement—a plan that retains the feeling of living in a traditional house and allows for the essential private bedroom and bathroom spaces. A style that was so American in origin, now takes on some quite unique French characteristics.

The French rarely seem to start decorating from scratch—nor do they ever consider a room finished. There is a persistent attitude that "it's just a matter of rearranging as one goes along."

The flea markets, nearly surrealistic arrays of furniture and knickknacks, are scoured relentlessly and imaginatively. "You don't care what it is, you just buy what you like, it's emotional," says one Parisian. That may well be true, but one talent that seems to be essentially Gallic is a sense of how to arrange the objects to their best advantage. There is not the more Anglo-Saxon need for everything to match.

On the contrary, the French seem to delight in the design surprise—shapes are contrasted, periods clash, colors are in striking and atypical combinations. And it all looks effortless, as if it had just been done and yet had always been there. What makes it most successful is its unerringly personal aspect.

"Europeans don't want their homes to look decorated," said Jean-Paul Beaujard, a French antiques dealer who has lived in New York for the past ten years; "it's all instinct."

Like the French woman, the quintessential French interior always looks put together as if by magic, projecting a thoughtful nonchalance, a refined elegance. It is composed without being self-conscious; a composition of shapes, a range of textures. It is quiet and serene without being dull; it can celebrate traditional values without being formal; it can be modern without being trendy. In the home, the French *joie de vivre* is a well-tempered *art de vivre*.

CITY LIVING

For both the French and the Francophiles, Paris has always been the city—the center, the heart, the soul—of the nation and the culture. Since the 19th century, it has been the very image of glamorous urban life, a model re-created in other urban centers in France, as well as around the world.

The grands boulevards of Paris and grandiose apartment buildings that lined the streets were conceived by city planner Baron Haussmann. They epitomize the bourgeois urban life in the same way that the apartments themselves, with their spacious rooms, winding corridors, and molding-encrusted ceilings embody the solidity and security of French urban life. But as in other cities whose architectural profiles have changed so drastically in the present century, Paris is absorbing a series of major design changes. The Centre National d'Art Georges Pompidou, known as the Beaubourg, has given the old Paris a high-tech injection, but for all of its modernism it has helped point up the endurance of its older neighbors.

Right: *The view of the rooftops of Paris, with small garret rooms hidden away under the eaves, is one of the classical images of the city.*

HOUSES

As anyone who has had the privilege of doing so can tell you, living in a house in the city is a special experience. But nowadays, in many cities and suburbs, one-family houses are rare.

Boston mansions, New York brownstones, and San Francisco Victorian houses have been divided into apartments and studios. And the same is true in London and Paris. Only a few examples of the grand hôtels particuliers built by the rich nobility in the 18th century and the large private houses of the wealthy bourgeoisie in the late 19th century and early 20th century have survived intact in Paris and the larger provincial French cities. Those that do remain are in the process of being renovated by new occupants who transform traditional settings into contemporary spaces.

Right: *A street in suburban Paris has a typical French mix of stone buildings and lush greenery.*

NEW ROMANCE, OLD WORLD CHARM

Monique Petit's suburban-Paris house is unabashedly romantic. Built in 1905, it had survived intact but neglected. Now it has been renovated by the antiques dealer, whose shop, La Pastorale, is in Paris's 16th arrondissement.

With the help of her daughter, Marie-Bernadette, and her son and son-in-law, both Beaux Arts architects, Petit has re-created the original feeling of Old World charm in the turn-of-the-century house.

Every room was meticulously furnished with antiques from the late 19th and early 20th centuries, but the interior is not in the least stuffy; rather, by introducing some modern pieces, she has avoided a museum atmosphere and created a comfortable, homey environment.

Above, right: *The stone facade of the turn-of-the-century house.*

Right: *A collection of antique canes is displayed just inside the front door.*

Top: *The garage is hidden behind a trompe l'oeil door on the street floor.*

Above: *Traditional French lace blinds hang from one of the second-floor windows over a sinuous wrought-iron grille.*

Above: *The flowered Liberty print fabric on the walls, the "Home Sweet Home" sampler, and the flowers in vases are part of the English feeling.*

Left: *In the paneled entrance foyer, straw hats and a faux bamboo table are a charming introduction to the tone of the interior.*

Left: *The contrast between the white painted walls, covered with cake-icing-like moldings, and the darker painted ceiling contributes to the success of the traditional room. The white china pots de crème, cups, and cachepots are pleasing, and suitably old-fashioned, accessories.*

Right: *The painted ceiling and the moldings in the graciously proportioned dining room were especially well preserved. The room has been furnished with a round dining table, unmatched antique chairs, and a pine armoire. A glass lighting globe hangs from the center of the ceiling. The original parquet floors are kept bare.*

Above: *The living room features a fireplace edged in antique tiles. A modern Italian leather sofa has been introduced among the pieces of antique furniture. Covered with a piece of white scalloped fabric, which acts as an antimacassar, it is an example of an unselfconscious decorating approach.*

Right: *Sepia drawings are part of one of the nostalgic still lifes in the house.*

Right: *At one end, the living room opens onto a magical grotto, a kind of winter garden that was often found in French houses of the era. Filled with plants and Victorian wicker furniture, it is one of the house's most Proustian environments.*

Below: *The elaborately carved wood mantel is topped with an antique rustic scene.*

Right and below: *Pieces of antique china, well-worn copper
pots, flea-market finds, and a collection of English and French jam
jars are displayed in the kitchen,
against a wall of pleasantly
cracked old white tiles.*

Below: *The kitchen, with its traditional French checkered floor, is
seen through the pantry door.*

Left: *A detail of one of the bath-rooms offers a glimpse of the antique green tile that covers the walls, a color that matches the rattan chair.*

Right: *The bedroom has a comfortable lived-in look. The bed, table, and chair are covered with white quilted fabric; an antique chaise sits by the fireplace.*

Below, right: *A window with painted glass panes opens onto the bathroom, a room that has been carefully accessorized—and includes a set of ivory-handled toilette articles grouped on the small wicker table.*

Below: *A flower-bedecked faience sink set on brass legs adds to the Old World quality.*

Left and below: *A two-sided iron staircase covered in ivy leads from the garden to the living room. The late-19th-century cast-iron furniture has a fern motif.*

TRANQUIL VILLA, SHARPLY DEFINED

It all began ten years ago when Maimé Arnodin and Denise Fayolle, who run Mafia, a large Parisian advertising agency, were seduced by a small iron staircase. They bought one of the houses in the "Villa Boulard," a group of 12 houses built under the Second Empire, half-hidden in an island of greenery, protected from the noise of the city. Paul Gauguin was among the artists who had lived in these houses, once considered modest residences.

The impeccable stone facade is white with shuttered windows. Andrée Putman designed the predominantly white-and-gray interior, combining original pieces from the Art Deco period with reproductions that reinforce the strict geometry of the spacious rooms. The glistening all-white bathroom was renovated a decade ago.

Below: *The dining room, with the kitchen hidden behind a partition, opens directly onto the garden. The floor is marble tile, the hanging lamps are Italian, and the high-back chairs are Thonet bentwood pieces.*

Right: *The typically French large square living room with tall windows and soft gray carpeting has been decorated in an Art Deco style. Two comfortable and over-scaled sofas are upholstered with men's suiting material. In the summer, they are slipcovered in loose ecru fabric. The table in the foreground is a reproduction of a Charles Rennie Mackintosh design; the 1930s bakelite object at center is more a piece of sculpture than a desk lamp.*

Below: *The fireplace, a mosaic of bits of mirror, is by the sculptor César. The lounge chair is a reproduction of Eileen Gray's Transat armchair.*

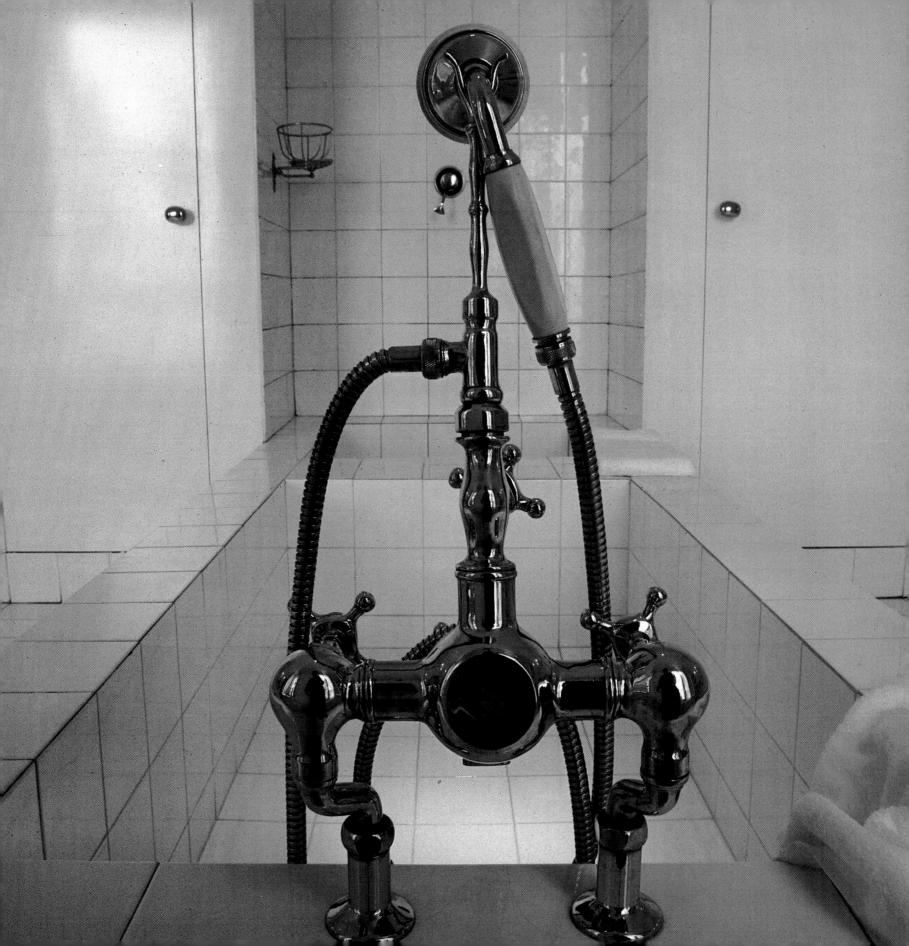

Left: *The design of the clinical-looking bathroom and the space given to it are unusual for a French home. Designed a decade ago by Andrée Putman, it features a centrally placed bathtub over which shines a spotlight, which gives it a warm glow and contrasts with the coolness of the white tile. The idea of placing sinks, one of which is situated at either end of the room, on tubular chrome legs was borrowed from London's Savoy Hotel.*

Below: *The heated wall-hung towel rack is like those found in hotels; the magnifying shaving mirror placed on a marble sink-top is an antique design.*

Above: *Italian white ceramic tiles cover the floor and the walls and are used for the bathtub. Although the faucets and hardware,* left, *look old, they are modern nickel-plated reproductions.*

Above: *The long radiator, a necessity in large, tiled bathrooms, was installed under the windows to rhythmically echo the pattern created by venetian blinds.*

VINTAGE FACADE, FRESH INTERIOR

In many cities in France during the last ten years there has been a revitalization of older neighborhoods and a resurgence of interest in the architecture of the 18th and 19th centuries. An outstanding example of renovation can be found in Bordeaux, one of the country's most important provincial cities, especially in the magnificent 18th-century buildings that surround the stock exchange near the piers.

These were once the homes of the wealthy spice, wine, and fish merchants, who lived above their shops. The house shown on these pages had been in shambles. The kitchen and bathrooms were modernized; and the spatial proportions, so reflective of 18th-century French architecture, were rediscovered.

Parisian architect Jean Pistre was sensitive to the original grand style of the house, and was able to strike a balance between its classic French lines and more modern furnishings. The pale beige-and-white palette he chose provides a youthful and contemporary finish for the classical details of the house.

Above: The facade of the 18th-century stone house has been cleaned and so stands out from its still-dark neighbors. The tall windows, ironwork, and stonework above the windows are typical of the period.

Right: The rhythmic winding staircase can be seen from the main courtyard.

Below: The 18th-century wrought-iron balustrade has been repainted in traditional blue gray.

Right: The spacious kitchen is the one completely modern room in the house. Yet the storage element derives from a peasant tradition, found in many regions of France, of using such structures to keep food out of the reach of animals. The floor is covered in local tiles, made from Gironde stone. White ceramic tiles, white walls, and white-painted ceiling beams, as well as the furniture by Alvar Aalto, the Finnish architect, contribute to the natural-hued country-style room.

Above: *The strong sun of the Bordeaux region is filtered through intricate wood shutters, and is then reflected in the ornate tarnished gold mirrors.*

Right: *The traditional, paneled living room exudes an air of serenity. The deep bergère armchairs were found in the family's attic. Some have been painted white and reupholstered in white canvas, others simply slipcovered. The modern painting above the mantel was commissioned from artist Jacques Martinez.*

Left: *A black Régence table makes a strong graphic statement against the blond wood paneling. On it, a still life is composed of a turn-of-the-century lamp, a crystal candlestick, bronze figurines, and a bowl of hydrangeas.*

Right: *Three white plates set simply on a mantelpiece become part of a classical French still life. The effect is based on a contrast of different textures—wood, brick, and china—all in the same brown-and-white color.*

Left: *In the elegant bedroom, two terra-cotta medallions, once used to decorate a building facade, are placed on the white stone mantel. A modern Italian lamp and an easy chair with ottoman, covered in a blowsy floral print, are two unusual elements in an otherwise stark interior.*

Below: *The dressing table is made of ash and encased in what was once the fireplace shaft.*

Left: *In the bathroom, small white ceramic tiles line the big square tub. The large glass-enclosed space is open to the adjoining bedroom. The white sinks and fixtures are from Vola.*

Right: *The glass window behind the bed looks into the shower alcove and bathroom.*

Right: *The bedroom is designed around an unusual curved-frame bed, which was made in the 1930s by local Bordeaux craftsmen. The antique pillowcases are trimmed in lace; the curtains are of canvas, and the shades were made from mosquito netting.*

IN KEEPING WITH A BOHEMIAN ATMOSPHERE

Dany Simon and Philippe Aghion live in one of Paris's most special and desirable spots—the "Villa Montmorency," a series of private houses near the Bois de Boulogne. In 1848 the huge piece of property was purchased by the Pereire brothers to be made into a train station for the railway that circled the city. The scheme never materialized, and a few years later the land was subdivided. Little by little, houses filled the park; between the two world wars the "Villa" was known for the celebrities who lived there—the actress Sarah Bernhardt and the writer André Gide, among others.

The renovation of the house took only a fresh but thorough coat of paint, a change of upholstery, the removal of a few pieces of furniture, and the introduction of some of the couple's favorite personal possessions—family hand-me-downs, their own artwork, and stacks of art books and magazines—to create a warm and slightly bohemian atmosphere.

Below: *The 19th-century house has an exterior of white stone and red brick.*

Far left: *A small terrace hangs over the garden and is used for alfresco breakfasts.*

Below, far left: *The lush garden, with its mismatched assortment of chairs, is only yards away from a heavily trafficked city street.*

Left: *A partition-screen of wood and raffia separates the dining room from the living room in a traditional French way, but can be opened to unify the two rooms. The chair and the screen were family hand-me-downs. The table lamp is by Isamu Noguchi, the Japanese-American sculptor. Heavy white canvas curtains are hung on simple wood rings.*

Below, left: *In the dining room, as in the other rooms, the parquet floors have been highly polished, but kept bare. The table is covered with a piece of white oilcloth. The 1930s chairs belonged to Philippe Aghion's parents.*

Below: *White ceramic tiles cover the fireplace in the dining room.*

Above: *An enclosed verandalike room extends from the living room. The antique mother-of-pearl and Chantilly lace fan in the glass case in the foreground belonged to Philippe Aghion's grandmother. Instead of curtains, ivy, an extra note of greenery, covers the inside of the windows at the back of the room.*

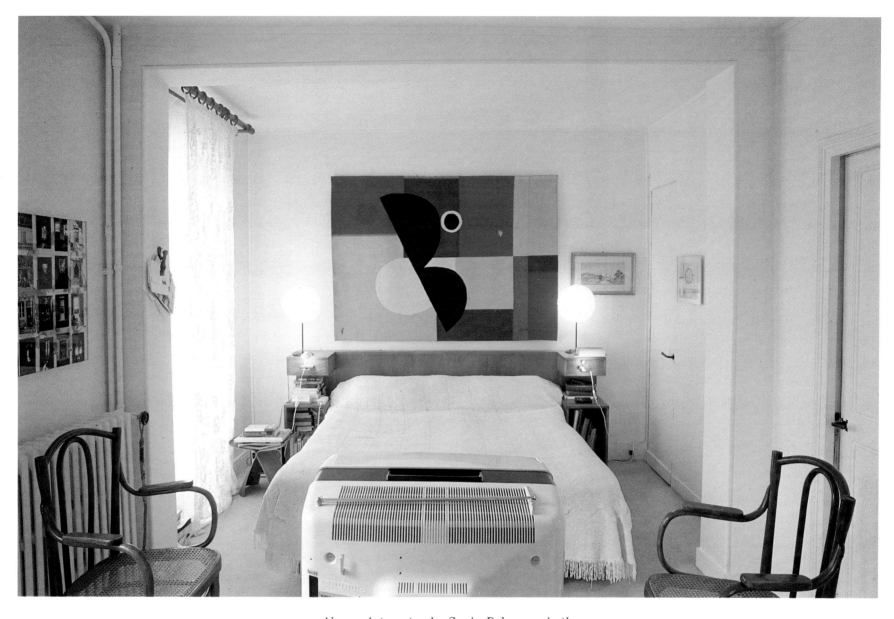

Above: *A tapestry by Sonia Delaunay is the only color in the white bedroom. Two Thonet bentwood chairs are placed on either side of the bed by the television set.*

TAMING EXTRAVAGANCE WITH HIGH STYLE

Many houses built near Paris in the 1930s were designed for a way of life that no longer exists. One of them, in Garches, about 25 miles from the capital, was once the residence of an Egyptian pasha and was designed by Auguste Perret, the architect who was also responsible for the Théâtre des Champs-Elysées.

It is an enormous structure with a gray cement facade and numerous windows, typical of the more imposing houses built in the Art Deco style.

Inside, the spacious rooms are more suitable to diplomatic receptions and large-scale entertaining than to intimate family life, and although the scale of the house was a deterrent to many prospective buyers, Emmanuelle Khanh, a fashion designer, and her husband, Quasar Khanh, a furniture designer, were seduced by its possibilities and decided to adapt it to their needs.

While retaining the aura of elegance typical of the building's architectural vintage, the renovation was able to tame the extravagance and bring it into a more livable scale without sacrificing the distinctly "grand hotel" flavor.

The Khanhs have not shied away from grandeur. There are sofas and chairs from the Art Deco period and unusual antique wicker mixed with modern pieces designed by Quasar Khanh.

Although disparate in style, the furniture coexists with unusual art objects created by the couple's numerous artist friends. Not only is the scale of these objects appropriately large, but each has been chosen in view of its color, texture, or evocative qualities.

Far left: *Emmanuelle Khanh in the entrance foyer; the oversized ceiling fixtures were in the house originally.*

Left: *The imposing 1930s house viewed from the garden steps.*

Right: *The "grand salon" with its paneled doors and majestic ceiling has been furnished with leather-covered chairs by Auguste Perret, the architect of the 1930s house, as well as an inlaid wood table by Quasar Khanh.*

Below: *Two polyester sculptures by Anthony Donaldson, an English painter and sculptor, stand in the vast front hall by the Art Deco staircase. The chandelier is Venetian and was designed for the residence.*

Bottom: *In the living room, the accessories include a 1930s rolling bar cart.*

Right: *An Art Deco chaise longue is uphol-stered in a traditional soft pink velvet usually reserved for more classical pieces.*

Far right: *Floor-to-ceiling doors separate the dining room from the living room. The vene-tian glass chandelier matches the one in the hall. The series of floor-to-ceiling doors leads majestically from one room to another and are reflected in the mirror over the mantel.*

Below: *In the upstairs hall, as elsewhere in the house, the bare parquet floors are covered with small rugs based on designs by contempo-rary or Art Deco artists.*

ATELIERS

When Gustave Courbet's Rue Notre-Dame-des-Champs atelier was depicted in a wood engraving in 1862, it caused a sensation in Paris by revealing that the realist painter brought live cows and bulls into the natural-light-filled and high-ceilinged space as models for his students. That atelier, however, was to remain an archetype of an artist's working environment. From then until the 1930s, Paris was an international center for artists, and many buildings were exclusively devoted to ateliers. They featured large-paned windows, often facing north, high ceilings, and a single main working-and-living space.

Many of these ateliers or studios have survived and are now prized by artists and nonartists alike. Their special qualities of light and unusual layouts, their mezzanines and generous footage, have ensured their enduring appeal. In Paris, ateliers are mostly to be found in Montparnasse and Montmartre, the areas where

such artists as Amedeo Modigliani and Pablo Picasso lived. Gertrude Stein, the writer and famous American patron of the arts, lived at 27 Rue de Fleurus, near Saint-Germain-des-Prés. Her studio, its walls covered with paintings, was a famous meeting place for artists in the first two decades of the century.

The modern efficiency apartment or studio and the whole concept of one-room living is a contemporary reflection of these splendid ateliers, but usually without the luxury of space or the architectural detailing of the 19th- and early-20th-century prototypes.

Right: *Large windows are one of the hallmarks of the atelier. This early-20th-century building has a tiled and ornamented facade.*

BAROQUE GRANDEUR ON A SMALLER SCALE

The huge 18th-century crystal chandelier is the focal point of the tiny high-ceilinged Parisian studio of Louise de la Falaise and her husband, Thadée Klossowski. It is located in a 1930s building originally built for artists.

When Louise de la Falaise, one of fashion designer Yves Saint-Laurent's associates, entertains, she turns off the electricity and lights the nearly 60 candles in the chandelier, re-creating on a small scale the sensual and glittering feeling of French court life.

It is luxury based not on lavish spending but on fantasy. A Louis XV bed, which would have been more at home in a boudoir, has been covered in antique fabric and serves as a couch in the center of the living room. Rich textiles are hung from the mezzanine, and full drapes unify the windows.

The sense of unreality is also heightened by the use of large-scale furnishings that were originally meant for vast château rooms and are surprising in this 1930s space.

The light blue carpeting used throughout adds to the dreamlike interior, anchoring it somewhere between the sea and the sky.

Above: *The large windows are a feature of the exterior of the 1930s artists' studio building.*

Above, right: *Brocaded and woven pieces of antique Chinese textiles are decoratively draped over the mezzanine railing.*

Right: *An antique bed is used in the center of the room as a freestanding sofa.*

Left: *A detail of the Italian rococo-style shell furniture, which, like the antique bed, has been adopted for its ornate and evocative qualities.*

Below: *The huge crystal chandelier dominates the high-ceilinged room.*

VARIATION ON A MINIMAL THEME

Some interiors are works of art, but few have been so deliberately planned for that effect as Jean-Charles Dedieu's Paris studio.

Dedieu sees himself as a theatrical director who sets the stage with people and objects. He had all the walls in his apartment torn down to produce a single clean, empty, open space in which to display his collection of conceptual art.

But while the studio was to act as a background for compositions of artworks and furniture, it also had to function as a place in which to live. An area for storage was built around a central structural column; the rest of the studio was left open. Dedieu had two low platforms designed: one for the daybed, the other for a group of photographs, sculpture, and decorative objects.

Dedieu has managed to translate the abstract qualities of the monochromatic paintings into a minimalist interior—not by eliminating all objects but by perfectly placing the ones selected.

Above: *The studio's planned composition of art objects includes a series of black-and-white photographs laid out on a low platform. Behind is a Brancusi vase and a César compression near an Italian black leather kneeling chair and a ponytail plant.*

Right: *On entering, one is confronted with the stark view of the back of the central column with three large conceptual paintings: one white, one black, one gray. The chair is a 1930s design.*

Left: *The other side of the column is used for storage and a small office. The neatly organized area has a cluttered look: Prints and photographs hung one atop the other, and objects layered on the shelves contrast with the minimalism of the studio.*

Below, left: *The small red-and-white kitchen is based on a Pop Art theme. Soup cans by Andy Warhol hang on the wall, shiny pots by Jean-Pierre Raynaud sit above the window—and the sink and stove match the art.*

Right: *The few pieces of furniture—a bed on a platform and two classic Le Corbusier chairs—are carefully placed, as if on a grid pattern, in the restructured space. The walls are white, the cement and sand floor is polished, and the windows are covered with venetian blinds. Ordinary materials—the mover's quilt on the bed, the plywood of the office walls—were chosen intentionally.*

FRANKLY INSPIRED BY ART AND CRAFT

It is appropriate that Madison Cox, an art student, lives in a 1930s building in the 14th arrondissement of Paris that was originally built as artists' studios.

Everything in the small apartment looks casual, from the drop of the billowing canvas curtains that separate the living room from the sleeping area to the comfortable-looking seating. But in fact, the interior is an example of refined French design, carefully constructed nearly to the point of abstraction.

The walls, for example, are covered in brown kraft paper. But this rather ordinary material has been applied with the fastidiousness usually reserved for gold leaf.

The furniture in the living room area includes a sofa and two armchairs, original Napoleon III pieces upholstered in rich antique tapestry.

One of the designers who influenced Cox, in his muted natural color scheme, high level of craftsmanship, and especially the juxtaposition of luxurious and plain materials, was Jean-Michel Frank, the French interior decorator whose work in the Art Deco period of the 1930s is just now being rediscovered.

Right: *In the living room, two tall wire topiary forms in terracotta pots flank the plush, tapestry-covered sofa. The black leather military camp bed, used as a chaise, belonged to the duke of Morny, the half brother of Napoleon III. The low oak screens that hide the radiators were inspired by Jean-Michel Frank.*

Above: *For privacy and a sense of intimacy,
the bed is placed in a small alcove and separated from the living room area with a series of
white canvas curtains. The same material was
used for the window shades. The floors are covered in natural sisal matting.*

Above: *One of the focal points of the interior is the way ordinary textures are played off against more luxurious ones—the leather of the camp bed against the wire of the topiary forms; the softness of the full canvas curtains contrasting with the stiffness of the light wood screens.*

INTERNATIONAL ARRANGEMENT

There are the French park chairs, which look plucked straight out of the Tuileries Gardens, the English Lloyd Loom cane chair, the Japanese sandals by the bed, the modern Italian table, the American pressed glass from the 1930s and 1940s, and the display rack of postcards. All hint at the international character of Anne-Marie Dubois-Dumée's small, bright, nearly all-white Parisian pied-à-terre.

Dubois-Dumée is a publicist who travels widely, and the Saint-Germain-des-Prés studio provides her with a place that is easy to come home to. The simple, informal, and open interior would be suitable to the life-style of any young working woman. The lounge chairs are loosely slipcovered, the slatted chairs fold for storage, and the Italian Archizoom table is plastic laminate.

It is a budget-minded approach that has been given a touch of Gallic style as well as humor—by the introduction of the gold chandelier, for example.

Right: *The bedroom is also a home office and is separated from the rest of the space by a sliding partition. A florist's plant stand is both headboard and bedside table. The American quilt provides a touch of color.*

Left: *Folding white chairs are used for dining around a large black-and-white Italian table. The floors are all covered in white ceramic tile.*

Below, left, and below: *The compact kitchen is open to the adjacent living-dining area, unusual in France, where kitchens are often kept separate from other rooms.*

APARTMENTS

The urban apartment house in France is a genre of residential buildings that encompasses a range of styles. Particularly in Paris, where neighborhoods developed at different times, it is not unusual to see facades of various architectural periods standing side by side—from the flowing sculptural details of the Art Nouveau period to the flat geometric fronts preferred by the modernists since the 1920s and 1930s.

By the second decade of the 20th century, a modern apartment building in Paris or an important provincial city could boast not only central heating but garbage disposals, bathrooms, and an elevator.

Few foreign visitors to France ignore the elevators—those fast-rising small cages with swinging doors and wood-paneled interiors, plus, not infrequently, a sign reading "En Panne." Many were put into the stairwells long after the buildings were completed.

In traditional apartments, the living and dining rooms often had balconies that faced the street; the bedrooms and kitchens were laid out along a corridor or looked out over an inner courtyard. Apartments in late-19th- or early-20th-century buildings were spacious and high-ceilinged, with fireplaces in every room despite the introduction of central heating. The most sought-after locations overlooked a city park.

There existed a certain ritual to entering these buildings. Pushing open the heavy front doors, one was momentarily blinded by the dimness of the ground-level entrance before proceeding past the ever-present concierge to reach the wide, winding staircase or enter the tiny elevator.

Today modern European apartment houses more closely resemble their American counterparts. In high-rise buildings the spaces are smaller, and the elevators are unfortunately less picturesque.

Right: *The view down the stairwell in an old-fashioned Parisian apartment house, which was probably installed after the building was completed.*

REGAL SPLENDOR: PALACE FOR ONE

A few years ago, Karl Lagerfeld, one of France's foremost fashion designers, decided to go back in time. He sold his collection of Art Deco furniture and objects and moved into the apartment wing of one of Paris's most exquisite 18th-century hotels particuliers. The suite of rooms of unusual splendor was a miniature palace, and just the right size for one person.

Lagerfeld approached the interior with the eye of a perfectionist, ensuring that the perfectly preserved rooms would have the same grand elegance they had in the past. But instead of filling them with furniture and objects, the designer selected a few choice Louis XV period pieces and placed them exactly as they would have been in an 18th-century interior.

The museum-quality Louis XVI bed, signed Jacob, and its canopy of rich French embroidered fabric are the apartment's crowning glory.

The glittering richness of the 18th century is translated in modern terms in the mirrored bathroom.

Above, far left: *Ornate doors open onto the bedroom.*

Above, left: *The stereo cassette player, on the arm of the bedside lamp, is a modern element in the classically appointed interior.*

Left: *Although the library is formally decorated, Lagerfeld feels comfortable enough to pile up books and magazines.*

Right: *The red billowing taffeta curtains in the dining room contrast with the rich gold-and-cream interior. For extra historical ambience, candles are lit on the mantel.*

Right and below: *The bathroom resembles a hall of mirrors. Neon lights are recessed and hidden behind frosted glass panels. The Greek marble bathtub, designed by Lagerfeld, and the sinktop contrast with the more industrial look of the rolling hospital table.*

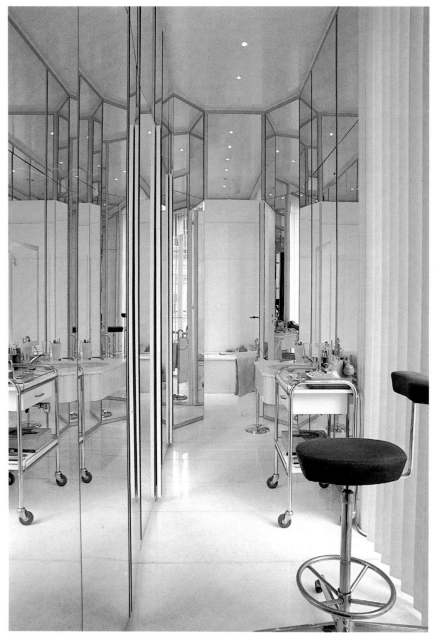

IN A TOWER
ON THE SQUARE

One of the current inspirations for modern French design is the white spaces championed by the architect Le Corbusier more than 40 years ago. All-white spaces have a serene classical feeling to them, and interior designer Estelle Lugat Thiebe's apartment in Amiens is a good example of how the design concept can work when it is based on the play of proportions and a strict sense of geometry. Situated on the 16th floor of a tower designed by the architect Auguste Perret in about 1950, the square space overlooks the train station. The design of the interior was based on the square plan of the building and laid out to take advantage of the windows, which offered views in four directions. The plan also allowed for the unusual layout: The sleeping, cooking, and storage areas are grouped around a central core.

Low partitions separate but do not close off the bedroom and the bathroom, while the kitchen and the laundry are isolated so that machinery noises are muffled. The few pieces of Charles Rennie Mackintosh furniture were chosen for the visual effect of their black frames standing out against the glossy white walls and the white ceramic tile outlined in black grout.

Above and left: *The tall tower designed by Auguste Perret overlooks the 13th-century Gothic cathedral, Amiens's most famous architectural landmark.*

Right: *The bedroom and bathroom are situated behind low partitions, beyond the open living and dining areas.*

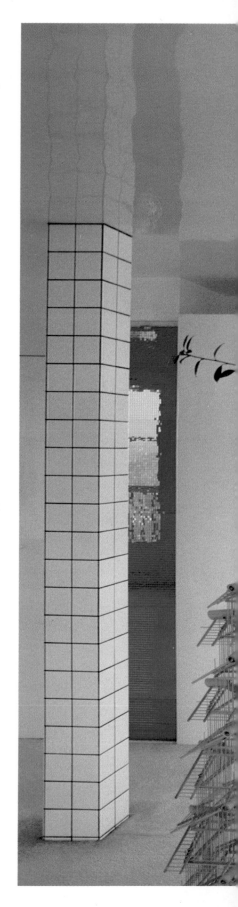

Left and below, left: *Two views of the dining area with black wood chairs that are reproductions of Mackintosh designs. The table is made of white ceramic tiles.*

Below: *A mandarin bird flies freely around and perches on one of the chairs.*

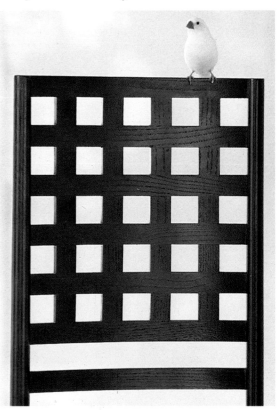

Right: *A potted amaryllis and a bowl of strawberries are the few touches of color in the black-and-white interior.*

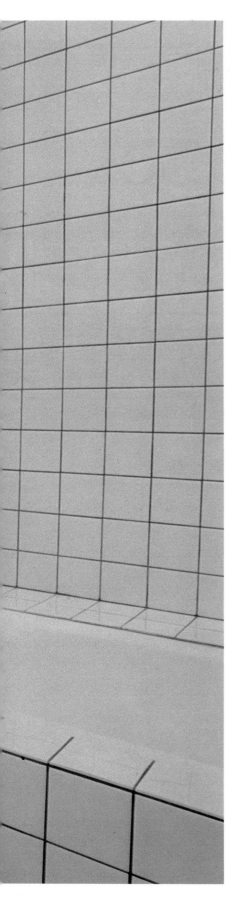

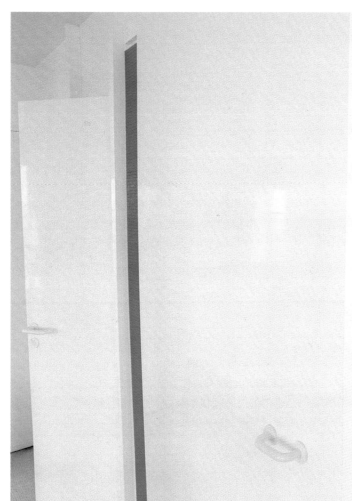

Above: *The small kitchen can be closed off behind a door to isolate its sounds and cooking odors from the rest of the space.*

Far left: *The white tile grouted in black is a design feature carried throughout the apartment. The bathroom is open to the sleeping area; the bedcover is made of black-and-white ribbon.*

Left: *A fawn sculpture reigns over a group of plastic geraniums set in clay pots.*

Left: *In the living room, which doubles as a studio, there is an assemblage of objects that are typical of the decorator: a 1930s sofa by Pierre Chareau, a pair of African ceremonial stools, and a carved 19th-century wood statue of an African child.*

Far left: *One of a pair of cubist paintings hangs over the ceramic fireplace; a collection of trompe l'oeil terra-cotta objects are arranged on the mantel.*

Left: *Through a screen sculpture by Kim Hamisky a niche filled with 1930s vases can be glimpsed.*

PAST AND PRESENT: AN URBANE MIX

Jacques Grange is one of the most respected of France's young interior designers. His understated style is based on an original interpretation of the past, particularly the late 19th and early 20th centuries. But rather than simply borrowing from these eras, Grange daringly combines antique furnishings with unusual pieces of modern art and his own esoteric finds.

The scale and ambience of his interiors recall the small paintings of rooms that were popular in Europe in the mid-19th century, and Grange sometimes places furniture as it was depicted in those paintings. The rooms thus not only have a certain authenticity but hint at his predilection for subtle drama.

The mix of objects relies on a contrast of natural and precious textures: terra-cotta and well-polished woods, plain white cotton and fine cashmere, lustrous glazed tile and the well-worn weave of a fine Oriental carpet, real African furniture and 19th-century Viennese carved statues of African children.

In his own Paris apartment, which has the air of both an English gentleman's private club and an elegant and urbane Frenchman's abode, there is a painterly play of light and shade. The bedroom and bathroom are done in muted tones; the living room is a light-filled, nearly flamboyant space.

Right: *A large canopy bed sculpture in the shape of a bird and a sleeping dog sculpture, both by François Lalanne, are also in the living room.*

Right and far right: *The intimate master bedroom, done in muted shades, recalls the atmosphere of postimpressionist Edouard Vuillard's paintings. The bedcover is made of antique cashmere; the carpet is Turkish; a screen acts as a headboard.*

Below: *The adjoining bathroom is also understated and refined. The tiles are from the 19th century, the pink flamingo is a 1900 lithograph originally from a bistro, and the chair is an antique rattan piece.*

Above: *In the living room, an inflatable blimp, new-wave paintings, and a folding striped umbrella chair contrast with the ornate, late-19th-century fireplace.*

A FORMAL FRAME, A WITTY STYLE

As in other cities, many young people in Paris, unable to afford the chic neighborhoods, are moving into areas that were once unacceptable.

The working-class and lower-middle-class neighborhoods that border the Saint-Germain-des-Prés and Montparnasse districts are the ones that hold a growing appeal. Olivier Gagnère, a lighting and furniture designer, is among the young urbanites who are new residents.

In a typical late-19th-century building in the 14th arrondissement, Gagnère found a two-room apartment with a tiny kitchen, and a bathroom in the outside hall. But it also offered high ceilings, elegant french windows, parquet floors, and an 1880s carved marble mantel.

Into this traditional frame, Gagnère injected his own cheerful and jaunty style—what he calls "a mixture of high-tech and tutti-frutti." It is a slightly irreverent approach that mixes humor with what Americans would recognize as a "punk" sensibility. Although personal, the design point of view is well understood by his budget-minded but style-conscious contemporaries.

The designer's own work includes the fluorescent tubular lights and a decorated chest inspired by Italian avant-garde designs.

Right: The walls and parquet floors have been painted white. Black metal venetian blinds, instead of curtains, cover the tall French windows.

Right: *Instead of hanging pictures and lamps on the walls, Gagnère prefers a less committed approach. In the bedroom, a painting leans against a wall and the fluorescent tube lighting he designed can be moved at whim. A perforated metal wall-hung shelf is the bedside table and bookshelf.*

Far right: *The black television set is on a skateboard for mobility; the telephone is installed on an extendable arm over the bed, and the invalid's walker near the window is used for clothing. The chest, a thrift-shop find, has been decorated and put on bright blue legs. The contrast between its bright pattern and the design of the American quilt is intentional and amusing.*

LUMINOUS DUPLEX: ROOMS WITH VIEW

Although Paris is not known for its tall buildings, there are some areas in the city that offer special views. But as modern Italian painter Valerio Adami and his wife, Camilla, discovered, even a Montmartre apartment can have windows that face an uninteresting street.

So the couple obtained permission to have square bays and round porthole-shaped windows punched out of the solid wall of the 1930s brick building. Now they can look out on not only the monumental baroque church of the Sacré-Coeur but a garden of tall trees and flowers and a typically French bowling green. The result—a light-flooded interior with a far-reaching view unusual for a Parisian apartment.

The duplex is reminiscent of the luxurious interiors of the French Art Deco period—the nautical accessories, the circular windows, and the original 1930s paneling accentuate the feeling of a grand prewar ocean liner. The choice of modern classical furnishings—a mirror by Emile-

Jacques Ruhlmann, an Art Deco master craftsman, and classic chairs by Charles Rennie Mackintosh and Le Corbusier—reinforce this feeling.

Into this luxurious frame the couple has introduced a collection of contemporary art, drawings by Fernand Léger, Joan Miró, and George Grosz, sculptures by Louise Nevelson and Alexander Calder, a relief panel by Saul Steinberg, and Adami's own paintings. Antique Chinese and Oriental carpets and an African statuette complete this personal, eclectic interior.

Left: *One of the round porthole-shaped windows installed to take advantage of the view of the church of Sacré-Coeur.*

Right: *The curving staircase descends into the luminous white-walled foyer with its shiny black floors. An antique sailing boat is displayed on a rectangular Le Corbusier table.*

Below: *Windows were punched out of the blank wall in the exterior of the 1930s building.*

Right: *The dining room is furnished with an oval table and chairs by Mackintosh. The painting on the wall and the portrait of Nietzsche are by Adami; the silver pitcher is Art Nouveau style.*

Below, right: *The paneling in the living room is original to the apartment. A wall of frosted glass panels is used to mask a courtyard view. Two leather lounge chairs and two chairs by Le Corbusier are placed back to back. The small bull standing on the antique Chinese carpet is by Alexander Calder.*

Below: *The simple copper-and-brick fireplace, dating from the 1930s, is recessed into the built-in wood bookcases.*

Left: *After the interior walls were removed, a structural column remained. With inset lighting and painted white, it provides a strong classical element in the dining room. The chrome ashtray hung on the wall was bought at a flea market but originally came from an ocean liner.*

Below, left: *The dining room has a predominantly black-and-white color scheme. The shape of the windows is repeated by the oval table, and the grid of the backs of the Mackintosh chairs is echoed by the rectilinear placement of the artworks.*

Below: *Three objects, three styles: a painting by Louis Cane, a contemporary French artist; a Mackintosh "Willow" chair; and patterned Oriental carpets.*

Below: *The bathroom is also a play of geometric shapes; the mirror over the sink and the window are the same size.*

Bottom: *On the top floor, the round window is in the bathroom and a bay window is hidden behind the white curtains. The bed has a leather frame. A column sits squarely in the center of the stepped-up entrance. Collectors' pieces—the dressing table and mirror are by Emile-Jacques Ruhlmann—are humorously played off against a plaster bust of Dante sprayed gold.*

Right: *Near the window a chess table, from a flea market, is topped with a 1930s lamp and flanked by two Italian chairs.*

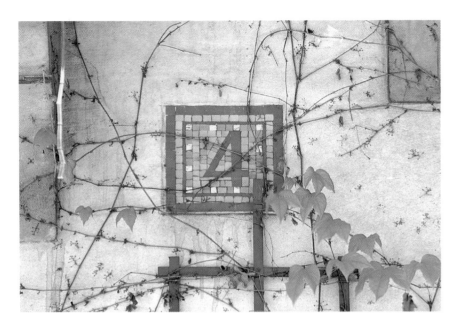

CONVERSIONS

In the annals of modern interior design, Americans earn the credit for pioneering the transformation of commercial lofts into residential spaces. It is an idea that has revitalized the old industrial areas of New York's SoHo, London's Covent Garden, and Paris's Les Halles.

But in adopting the concept, the French have gone their own way. Although recycled schools, churches, garages, and warehouses seen abroad have been an important influence, French designers undertake conversions with a unique approach. The results include some singularly refined interpretations of the high-tech aesthetic and subtle variations on traditional layouts for houses and apartments.

In Paris, much of the loft activity is centered in the areas of Les Halles and La Bastille, historically the site of small industries and light manufacturing concerns. And in many French cities, buildings that had remained empty for decades have been brought back to life.

The French are quickly adapting to the residential possibilities these once-unlivable structures offer. And if Paris lacks the architectural luster of New York's cast iron, it more than makes up for it in brick, tile, and wood.

Right: *The large windows, stone walls, and metal beams of these late-19th- and early-20th-century factories and warehouses are typical of the buildings now being converted to residential use.*

DESIGN AND FORM: AN OBJECT LESSON

For 18 years, Andrée Putman felt as if she were in Alfred Hitchcock's movie *Rear Window*, intimately observing from her own apartment the activity in a seemingly thriving vacuum bottle factory.

The loft space under observation was in what the interior designer called "an accident," a late-19th-century building erected in the courtyard behind a 17th-century Paris residence. But suddenly the industrial concern went bankrupt, and because Putman had so long been an avid observer she knew about it before anyone else—and pounced on the space.

"It was a breath of oxygen in my life," recalled Putman, who for years has been a figure in the avant-garde of the Parisian design world. Her company, Ecart International, reproduces furniture from the 1920s and 1930s.

"I have always rejected colors," she said, of the almost totally black-and-white interior. In it she places the unusual and dramatic objects that attract her because of their interesting silhouettes, textured or mirrored surfaces, and potential for symmetry. Putman opted to keep the loft space open and has developed it in her own design style. Although the clean white walls and the graphic quality of the interior recall some of the visual drama of interiors of the 1930s and 1940s, Putman's approach is as original as it is personal.

And because she felt "there was not one area in the loft that would not have been destroyed by closets," Putman hangs her clothes out in the open on old department store racks. The garments, which are predominantly black and white, become part of the aesthetic of the whole.

Far left: *Because the loft is on the top floor, it is flooded with light from a skylight. The chrome-and-black chaise by the architect Le Corbusier is one of the classic modern pieces of furniture favored by Putman.*

Left: *The objects that line one wall of the loft are an indication of the range of the designer's interests. The 18th-century German clock is made of mirror etched to represent clusters of grapes; the desk is an Art Deco black lacquer piece with ivory inlays; the carpet, called Blackboard, is by the 1920s designer Eileen Gray and produced by Ecart.*

Below, left: *In the 1960s, Putman designed two small mirrored commodes and had them custom-made. The 19th-century carved wood chairs with their representations of sphinxes have been reupholstered in horsehair. Of indeterminate origin—English, Venetian, or French—they once belonged to Sarah Bernhardt, the famous actress.*

Right: *There are no interior partitions in the loft space. Furniture is placed against the walls or in relation to the strong verticals created by the metal beams.*

Below and bottom: *The bedroom has been installed in an L-shaped alcove in the loft. The bed, placed on a low platform, is separated from the rest of the space by a series of panels of fiber glass mosquito netting hung from a track. The sheer fabric allows the bed to be enclosed and private, yet lets light into the area.*

98

Left: *Antique Thonet bentwood chairs and a settee surround a mirrored table from the 1930s on which are displayed a Bakelite lamp from the period and a baroque object in bronze. On the wall is a dramatic triptych by Françoise Jourdan-Gassin.*

Top, right: *Ecart reproductions of a René Herbst chair form another grouping in front of the windows. The tea service with a samovar and a large piece of pottery by Pierre Culot are part of this vignette.*

Center, right: *A greenhouse was installed to serve as a summer dining room and has been furnished with a bistro table and bentwood chairs by Le Corbusier and Thonet.*

Bottom, right: *The landscaped roof garden is shielded to provide a protected environment for plants that might often be seen in a southern climate.*

101

REDESIGN COURSE: SCHOOL INTO HOME

In 1975, when Eric and Xiane Germain returned to Paris from a trip to the United States, they began searching for a place to live where they could experiment more freely with space and apply some of the design ideas they had seen abroad.

The Germains discovered a building near the Eiffel Tower that had once been the site of the Cours Montalembert, a proper girl's school that had closed in the 1950s. It provided them with the opportunity to recycle an old commercial building, in this case a school, into residential use. The couple hired Michel Boyer to do the renovation, which included the installation of a heating system and an industrial cement staircase.

Eric had lived for many years in Algeria and had never lost his taste for the white rooms that are so especially refreshing in the summer. Xiane, influenced by the Bauhaus movement in architecture and design, also liked open, rather empty spaces. Both were interested in painting, photography, and architecture; they wanted a sober house that would provide an understated background for experimental artworks and where their many artist friends would feel at home.

Right and below: *Philippe Sorensen created an unusual botanic garden on the site of the former schoolyard. The building's brick facade is now completely covered in Virginia creeper; the walks and steps are paved with granite. There is a profusion of flowering plants in the garden—many rarely seen in Paris.*

Left: *The color scheme of the understated living room is limited to off-white and black. The room is furnished with classic modern pieces—including a plastic shell chair by Joe Colombo, the Italian designer—and African sculptures and functional objects.*

Far right: *The placement of furniture and objects along a geometric grid is indicative of the classical modern decor.*

Right and below: *Rodin sculptures and a Lalique glass bowl are on the black wood commode, which is flanked by two chairs by Jean-Michel Frank.*

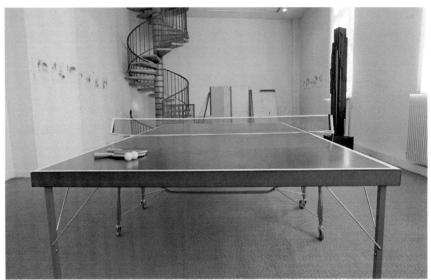

Far left: *The Germains like to leave tables uncluttered. In the dining area, an Alvar Aalto table with modern Italian chairs is next to the industrial cement spiral staircase. Four black-and-white photographs hang on the wall; an African funerary urn sits in front of the stairs.*

Left: *The game room on the second floor is equipped for table tennis. The room is sometimes used as a gallery for friends' paintings and photographs.*

Below, left: *A blond wood Alvar Aalto stool and a drafting table are used as a small work area near the windows.*

Far left and left: *African sculptures, a textile work, simple canvas chairs, and a television set are all displayed together and illustrate the Germains' unselfconscious approach to freely mixing objects from varied cultures and of differing values.*

Below, left: *In a second-floor bedroom, the white-tiled bathroom is hidden behind a sliding door partition system. The white cotton voile panels framed in black ebony give the room its Japanese feeling. Two 1930s lamps stand on the bamboo bedside tables.*

Right: *A white slatted bench by American designer Harry Bertoia serves as a base for an African statue and a series of wood sculptures by Jean-Michel Bertholin.*

A VERTICAL LOFT ON THREE LEVELS

In 1977, Daniel Rozensztroch, a housewares buyer and stylist, embarked on a pioneering real estate endeavor. He joined a group of friends in converting a dusty and empty woodworking factory into residential co-op loft spaces.

The building is in the Faubourg Saint Antoine neighborhood, an area of warehouses that has been known since the 18th century for its small industrial workshops.

Christian Gimonet, the architect who was in charge of the renovation, came up with an unusual plan for the spaces. Rather than cutting them up horizontally, he divided the brick building on the vertical. Each of the tenants was then free to design his own interior.

Rozensztroch opted for a modern scheme—"my own interpretation of French high-tech," he calls it. It is a bright, primary-hued modern interior on three levels. "I didn't want to live in a big, open loft," he added. "In France, we have a notion of the house to which we're attached." A winding stair connects the three floors. The bedrooms are on the ground floor, the main living area and kitchen are in the center, and a cantilevered work space occupies the top floor.

For materials and accessories, Rozensztroch chose both classic objects and products from industrial sources, but kept to primary colors, white, and black. "My way of getting back to basics," he said.

Left: *The large main living space is on the middle level. Instead of being open to the dining area, the kitchen is shielded behind a greenhouse-type glass enclosure, which lets it remain visually open yet ensures that cooking odors and noise are kept away from the dining area.*

Below: *The brick building, once a woodworking factory, was planned around a center courtyard now converted into a shared garden for the co-op.*

Left: *The third-floor study offers a bird's-eye view of the dining area. The classic bentwood chairs have been painted black; the plates, with their primary-colored borders, are from Hong Kong. Metal factory shades are hung over the dining table.*

Left: *A modern Danish wood-burning stove, chosen both for functional and aesthetic reasons, is set on a white-tiled floor facing the living room area.*

Right: *The winding, tiled staircase connects the three levels of the loft. Rozensztroch, a design perfectionist, had the tiles laid so that their lines matched up exactly.*

Below: *The study-work area of the upper level is cantilevered over the open living area.*

Left: *Typically French, the kitchen is small but well organized. Instead of being hung on brackets, the industrial wire shelving is set into the wall. The shelves are placed one in front of the other instead of above one another, allowing kitchen equipment to hang freely. The plastic faucets and sinks, manufactured by Vola, and the stovetop are set into a black plastic laminate counter. The wall lights are similar to those traditionally used in cellars.*

Right: *In the bedroom, on the lower floor, there is space only for the bed and a shelf that doubles as a headboard. Greenhouse glass is used for an interior window.*

Below, right: *The bathroom is small and simple, with white tiles, primary-colored fixtures, and a chair by René Herbst.*

115

LOFT ON MODIFIED AMERICAN PLAN

Although recycling factory space for residential use is still relatively rare in France, such Parisian neighborhoods as the Bastille have begun to follow the pattern of New York's SoHo area. As small industrial concerns disappear, the newly available buildings are being converted for use as homes.

The one chosen by Stan Levy, an art director, was totally unlivable when he asked Andrée Putman and Jean-François Bodin to plan its interior architecture. Both the designers and their client had been impressed by the American concept of the loft as a vast open space and hesitated to close off any of its areas. But finally a more European sense of space prevailed. While the kitchen, living, and dining areas were left open, the bedrooms and bathrooms were enclosed for privacy.

The loft is a high-tech interior, a space in which the furnishings are from industrial or commercial sources. Many existing industrial elements were incorporated into the design: the exposed steel beams, which are the French equivalent of the American cast-iron columns; the refinished hanging factory lights; and the wall of factory windows, which gives the loft its special quality of light.

But the look has been tempered so that one is not overwhelmed by the bravura of using industrial materials. Rather it is a subtle, elegant interpretation, in which the high-tech elements are kept on a more sober scale and made to work with more traditional design features.

To this the designer has added her own luminous, elegant detailing. In the kitchen, for instance, the paint used is one in which there are suspended particles of color. The overall color scheme was kept to white, black, and gray, with touches of bright blue in the Eileen Gray carpet, the dishes, and especially the refined use of mosaic in the white-tiled bathroom.

Right: *Facing the wall of factory windows, the kitchen and the dining area of the loft are kept completely open. The floors are covered with gray commercial carpeting or small square ceramic tiles in a matching color. The rug in the foreground is a reproduction of an Eileen Gray design called La Méditerranée.*

116

Left: *In the modern, American-style kitchen, high chairs are pulled up to a tiled counter for informal meals. The undercounter storage cabinets have wire-mesh glass doors.*

Right: *Stainless steel sinks are set into the kitchen work counter. The hanging factory light, although original to the space, was completely refinished. Books, magazines, and stereo equipment are kept on a series of industrial bakers' racks along one wall of the loft. The enclosed bathroom is at the rear of the space.*

Below, right: *The kitchen is equipped with a wall-mounted oven, as well as a television set.*

Far right: *The dining table, an Ecart design, has a thick, frosted glass top and a chrome base on casters. It is surrounded by four American metal porch chairs from the 1950s.*

Above: *The original structural steel metal "columns" have been painted white and incorporated as a decorative geometric element in the loft. A two-sided fireplace divides the living room area from the small work area. The furniture includes a set of original Josef Hoffmann pieces, right, and a modern chair of blue baked enamel by Sacha Ketoff.*

Above: *The bathroom, a separate room, has a metal frame and glass door and clerestory that echo the design of the loft's factory windows. A piece of fabric, used by photographers as a reflective material, is thrown over the sofa.*

Above: *Including the shower enclosure, the bathroom is entirely covered in shiny white ceramic tile. A strip of electric blue mosaic tile set in the floor near the tub delineates an imaginary bathmat, and recalls the blue-and-white towel design traditional to hotels.*

Above: *The strip of blue mosaic tile is repeated along the edge of the shower, which is also covered in square white tiles.*

COUNTRY LIVING

There are few landscapes that can so quickly conjure up such pleasant and seductive thoughts as the French countryside. Varied in topography and climate, the bucolic areas of France each have their own charm and attributes, as well as their own regional architectures. The tiled roofs of Provence, the rugged towns of Brittany, the age-old stone houses of the Massif Central—these are the areas that the French hold so close to their hearts no matter where they live or where they spend their vacations.

Country houses in France run the gamut from rustic to sophisticated, from simple to grandiose. But always, there still remains a respect for the past in the renovation or modernization of these homes. The large brick fireplace, the stone floors, the stuccoed walls, all represent the endurance of the past into the present.

Right: *A view of the medieval Provencal town of Gordes and its terraced houses with their thick walls that are a protection against the heat and wind.*

HOUSES

The urban French, like their American counterparts, dream of finding the perfect country house. Situated in a forgotten village, down an untrodden path, or completely hidden in a forest, the house is an embodiment of the ideal of a simpler way of life—subsisting off the soil, retreating from urban crowds and pressures to the slower pace and firmer values of the past.

Some people are able to return to the homes of their parents; others set down new roots in acquired properties. But in France as elsewhere, fewer and fewer areas remain to be discovered, and the houses grow less affordable. However, in more remote and sparsely populated rural areas, barns or houses, with roofs of tile, slate, or thatch and walls of stone or stucco, are still available at moderate prices for those willing to renovate from scratch.

Country houses in France can range from the primitive to the elegant, but all tend to exhibit a respect for the local materials and architectural styles.

ELEGANT MANOR, COUNTRY CHARM

One of France's most ancient regions is the Touraine, a province southwest of Paris, which is known for its castles, its wines, and its mild climate. It is there that Pacha Bensimon, an advertising executive, lives in a house whose foundations date back to 1540.

The manor house, hidden among 100-year-old trees, had been empty since the French Revolution, although it had been rebuilt in the 18th century.

The facade presents the formality typical of the French manor houses of the period, but the interior has none of the stiffness one might expect to find behind such walls. The furnishings are mostly antiques; the armoires, sideboards, and doors run a gamut of styles spanning the centuries since the house was built.

It is a typical old French country house full of young ideas that would be just as at home in a less grand setting. The front vegetable garden, planted where a rigorously laid out flower garden might be expected, hints at the warm informality inside.

Above: *The gentle Touraine landscape as seen through the arched windows of the house.*

Right: *The facade of the manor house has been covered with a beige-colored mixture of earth and sand of the Loire. The traditional vegetable garden produces food for the household.*

Left: *The doors in the house, although refinished, are original, as are the ceiling beams. In the hall, a series of doors placed next to one another lead to the bedrooms.*

Below, left: *An enormous branch of mistletoe, traditional for New Year's, hangs in the hall throughout the year. While the walls have been reworked with colored sand, the floors are simply faded and worn with time.*

Right: *One of the bedrooms achieves a nearly monastic serenity. The walnut-framed bed is covered with an Irish coverlet; the walls are decorated with bunches of grasses and heather that recall the surrounding countryside.*

Left: *Although each of the plates on the dining table is different, and some are even chipped, they form a satisfying composition. In the back, the kitchen with its antique stove is open to the room.*

Below: *An arrangement of holly adorns a corner of the living room's late-18th-century mantel.*

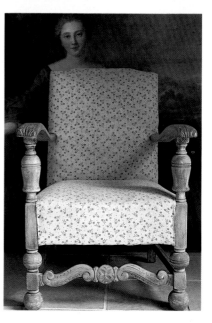

128

Above: *The large living room is sparsely furnished with a few overscaled pieces. The chairs, including an 18th-century-style wing chair,* far right, *have been stripped and reupholstered in country-style printed fabric.*

Left: *A reproduction Renaissance chair is put illusionistically in front of an antique painting.*

Above: *In a bathroom, the walls are tinted deep rose. The fixtures were bought locally, and the oval mirror above the sink is from an old hat-making establishment.*

Left: *The exterior of one of the old claw-footed bathtubs has been painted for a trompe-l'oeil marble-like effect. The antique cane folding chaise was originally a lounge for invalids.*

Far left: *An old coat rack is used to display a collection of antique country jugs.*

ON THE SURFACE: CHINA AND SHELLS

As a sculptor, César Baldacini has glued, assembled, compressed, and expanded a variety of materials—including iron, paper, wood, glass, and plastic, to transform ordinary elements into eloquent and powerful works of art.

Another side of the artist's personality emerges in his peaceful house on the French Riviera, a region that for decades has been a favorite of artists. César was born in Marseilles, and his stuccoed house near Saint Paul de Vence is a reflection of a more languorous, typically Mediterranean style.

The totally original way he has decorated the house is another kind of assemblage—less violent than many of his artworks, but no less baroque in its mixture of styles and its graceful clutter.

César is an inveterate habitué of the local flea markets. After many years of accumulating ceramics, shells, and 19th-century bentwood furniture, the artist discovered that these disparate objects seem to settle in together and become part of a whole. The kitchen and the bathroom in particular show the artist's extraordinary manipulation of different materials.

Above, left: *In many of the rooms, the furniture looks haphazardly placed—a typically French approach for flea-market finds.*

Left: *The white-walled living room is furnished with 19th-century bentwood and a screen.*

Right: *A wicker chair filled with seashells is one of the artist's baroque accumulations of objects.*

César borrowed the extraordinary technique of embedding broken bits of china and mirror in plaster—an approach inspired by certain 19th-century planters and umbrella stands and reminiscent of the exuberant and marvelous Park Güell in Barcelona, by Antonio Gaudí, the turn-of-the-century Spanish architect.

In the kitchen, left, and detail, top right, *the color scheme of the tiling is kept mainly to white; multicolored bits, top, far right, become a bedroom headboard; pink pieces of china are used in powder room, far right; and blue flowered bits are part of ceiling fixture frieze, right. In the master bathroom, below, pieces of mirror are added to white tile chips to make walls shimmery.*

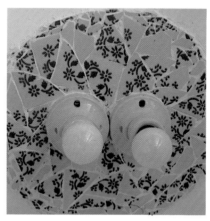

REGIONAL HOUSE, WELL-WORN STONE

When Marc Held, a designer of modern furniture and accessories, wants to escape with his family to the country, he goes to a rented house in the center of France.

The Corrèze, or "green country," is in the province of the Limousin and has become known since World War II for cattle raising.

Built not long after the French Revolution, on the ruins of an ancient castle, the house is believed to have belonged originally to a wealthy family. But by the end of the 18th century it had become the model for the local peasant abodes. Today, it is in many ways characteristic of the region—with its superb chestnut building frame, its walls grouted with earth, and its stone floors worn smooth by cobbled boots and clogs.

The living functions of the house center around the "cantou," an enormous fireplace in the main room that in the past was used not only for cooking but also for heating and drying clothes.

Held has integrated modern conveniences and furnishings into the ancient building. It is an informal, unpretentious home that still retains the essential characteristics of its unsophisticated past.

Above, left and left: *The Held family eats outdoors in front of the house with its earth-grouted walls and shuttered windows.*

Right: *A modern dining table dominates the main living space and contrasts with the ancient stone floors.*

Far left: *The walls of the renovated barn are made of stones from the region.*

Left: *In the large main living area with exposed beams the furniture includes a four-poster Louis XIII bed placed at one end of the room.*

Below, left: *There is a daybed in the main room to accommodate extra guests. The shelves inset in the wall are laden with local ceramic platters and pottery.*

Right: *Huge earthenware containers, full of bunches of lavender, are placed on the tile floor in front of the arched windows. The table is covered with a cloth of local patchwork.*

Below: *A butterfly is fixed on a plaster bust set on a cloth-covered side table near the entrance door.*

Above: *Each of the wood cabinets is filled with favorite objects made by local craftsmen.*

Right: *In a corner, a collection of bottles surrounded by bunches of dried field flowers provides a lyrical French country still life.*

Far right: *Visitors and family tend to congregate in the large kitchen, where stairs, walls, and fireplace are made of the red stone typical of the region. The table and chairs are simple country items, and baskets and bottles are mixed with peasant wares. The wrought-iron insignia on the wall is from a local blacksmith's forge.*

A LIFETIME OF COLLECTING: ONE MAN'S PRIZES

Few examples of a cultured and highly sophisticated French sensibility can compare with the house of Jean Lafont. Located in the marshy Camargue region in the south of France, the house is an impeccable portrait of its owner, who selected it 18 years ago because of the way it was situated behind tall plane trees, which keep it cool. Lafont raises bulls for "corridas," bullfights in which the bull is treated as a hero rather than put to death.

Although Lafont has unexpectedly punctuated one wall of the stuccoed exterior of the quiet country house with an unusual greenhouse veranda, it is the interior that is truly extraordinary.

Lafont has furnished the house with the rare objects he has collected for decades. Every piece—whether the intricately carved romantic Gothic chairs, the simple shapes of 1930s Art Deco furniture, the translucent Emile Gallé glass, or the muted harlequin pattern of 19th-century tiles—has been perfectly displayed in rooms each devoted to a particular period.

The house is not simply a repository of museum-quality objects but an example of one man's taste, based on a thorough knowledge of historic styles adapted to his particular passions.

Far left, top, center, and bottom: *Views of the exterior of the traditional stuccoed house, with a small relief of a bull over a door.*

Above, left: *The glass-enclosed veranda was designed by the artist César.*

Left: *A wood table and benches are near the veranda for alfresco dining.*

Right: *The veranda was custom-built for the ceramic Art Nouveau table and chairs from Sèvres, the famous porcelain and pottery center.*

Left: *The master bedroom is devoted to Lafont's collection of Gothic romantic furniture. A series of chairs stand on a 19th-century petit-point rug that depicts an imaginary and extravagant Gothic cathedral.*

Right: *A table set on the landing is used to display antique silver accessories. Overlooking the floor below is a huge 1900 lighting fixture designed by the French architect Pierre Selmersheim.*

Below, right: *In the master bath the wood paneling and the iron side chairs are in the Gothic style. The oval marble bathtub is from the 19th century.*

Above: *One of the guest rooms features a 1930s decor and includes a bed by Pierre Chareau, as well as pieces by Jean-Michel Frank. A series of photographs, including a portrait of Marie-Laure de Noailles by artist Man Ray, are hung like paintings along two walls.*

Above: *Another guest room has an Art Nouveau theme, with William Morris wallpaper, and a turn-of-the-century china mantelpiece.*

Left: *Adjoining the Art Nouveau bedroom is a bathroom whose bath enclosure is covered in 18th-century multicolor tiles set on the diagonal. Adjacent to the bathtub is a vitrine filled with Gallé glass pieces whose colors harmonize with the tilework.*

Right: *A smooth oval sandstone tub is at the center of another bathroom with a 1930s look. The dressing table and stool are by Louis Majorelle; the walls are paneled in wood. The stone floors are original to the house.*

ADDING A TOUCH OF THE EXOTIC

It is always a challenge to make an old house livable again without losing its essential character. So it was only after much deliberation that Chantal Thomass, a fashion designer, and her husband, Bruce, decided to take over a 1900 gray-stone house in Monfort-l'Amaury, about 25 miles from Paris.

The house, with its pointed roof, was large and curious, but Thomass had admired it since she had begun going to the country as a child.

The couple was attracted to the house by the fact that much of the original woodwork and detailing remained, including the tiled fireplaces and the parquet floors. "I like old houses," Thomass explained. "I find in them a certain quality of craftsmanship impossible to equal today."

Into the period house Thomass introduced some things that she especially liked because they were also well made—antique lace tablecloths and embroidered fabrics, for example. But she added an unusual exoticism that is reflected in the gold-leaf painting by Armand Colin.

All the woodwork was stripped, and the spacious rooms were furnished with comfortable sofas and a collection of antique faux bamboo cherry wood tables and chairs. The rich carved honey-colored wood contributes to the warm atmosphere of the interior.

Above: *The exterior of the gray stone 1900 house is partially covered with greenery.*

Right: *Dining chairs in faux bamboo and large sofas and chairs upholstered with heavy tapestry fabric are in keeping with the scale of the house and its rich brown-and-gold color scheme.*

Above: *The tall mirror and the tiled fireplace are original to the house. Lalique glass vases are displayed on a faux bamboo table.*

Right: *The coffered wood ceiling and the wall paneling and window frames were stripped and lightened. In a corner of the living room the Thomasses used old-fashioned flowers, lupines and delphiniums in purple and lilac, to emphasize the feeling of nostalgia.*

Above, left: *One of the bedrooms has been furnished with an antique bed. The wallpaper matches the hand-blocked Souleiado Provençal fabric used for the bedcover.*

Above: *Chantal Thomass keeps her collection of accessories and jewelry in a glass-topped table in the dressing room. Shelves of clothing are reflected in the mirrored doors of the elaborately carved wood armoires.*

Left: *Above the stairs on the landing a half-open door reveals a large 19th-century symbolist painting, which came with the house.*

Above: *The stove hood that runs the length of the kitchen wall has been covered with tiles from an old bakery. The spice rack was found in an Amsterdam flea market. The cherry wood chairs and marble-topped bistro table are antiques, but the tile floor is new.*

Above: *The large bathroom with its centrally placed tub combines old and new elements. The ornate wall tiles, the double sink, and the footed bathtub are original to the house, but the lights over the sink are reproductions.*

CHATEAUS

The grand French châteaus, for centuries the residences of the privileged, have an undeniably romantic appeal. The Loire Valley, Orléans, Tours, Blois, Chambord, and Chinon were especially favored by French kings and noblemen. But châteaus of notable architectural quality are scattered throughout the country, and a few are still in private hands.

Inherited from family or acquired at enormous expense, the castles often have problems—overgrown gardens, huge, empty ballrooms, and impossible-to-heat banquet halls—that their owners have neither the patience nor the funds to solve.

But, for those with the means and the imagination, there is little doubt that the magnificence of these historic structures can be revived. Whether restored or renovated, furnished with antiques or more modern pieces, these buildings can come to life once again.

FRENCH CLASSIC, ITALIAN ACCENTS

It is hard to imagine a French château more Italianate than the one built by the baron of Castille in the south of France.

The eccentric 18th-century castle, in disarray and surrounded by an overgrown garden, presented a decorating challenge. Its current owners asked Dick Dumas, an interior decorator who was formerly an antiques dealer, to undertake its renovation.

Imaginative and eclectic, Dumas was able to imbue the imposing residence with both decorum and humor. His taste for the flamboyant and his ability to pair modern art with unusual antiques was eminently suited to the task at hand.

The exterior of the building, including the imposing elliptical colonnade, was inspired by the work of the Italian baroque architects Andrea Palladio and Gian Lorenzo Bernini. But Dumas did not limit his design of the interior and the terraces to the classic Italian styles.

Instead he decided to give the castle its own identity by mixing furnishings from different classical periods—Roman, Greek, Egyptian, and Etruscan.

Colorful fabrics are used on the walls, country-style French furnishings are played off against the more formal architecture, and the result is a surprising mix of urbane sophistication and provincial casualness.

Right: *The neoclassic colonnaded entrance to the late-18th-century château was its original owner's idea of classical splendor.*

Left: *In 1962, Pablo Picasso created a mural for the loggia by embedding black stones in the white cement exterior walls.*

Right: *View from the loggia to the Italian-style garden, which was designed with low stone parapets and clipped shrubbery.*

Below, right: *Dumas decorated the dining room as a Turkish fantasy. Rusticated wood chairs are used around a modern table.*

AN OPEN HOUSE, A HISTORIC HOME

In the department of Yvelines, near Paris, Paul de la Panouse and his American wife, Annabelle, are revitalizing a château that has been in the viscount's family for 13 generations. Built in 1564, the castle belongs to the count de la Panouse and is listed as a historic monument that is open to the public. In 1968 the grounds were transformed into a zoological garden, and part of the château was turned into a museum. Six hundred thousand people visit it each year.

The family lives in another part of the château, and the viscountess is busy restoring, decorating, and planting, choosing furniture, laces, and paintings from the castle's many attics, and looking at local auctions for the overscale pieces needed to furnish the large rooms.

While the castle is one of the country's most precious repositories for many rare and historic books and letters, its interiors are neither formal nor intimidating. As it has for generations, the Château of Thoiry remains a lively family home.

Top, center, and below left: *The grounds around the 16th-century castle have been transformed by the viscount de la Panouse into a zoological garden, to which visitors come to see camels, giraffes, monkeys, and elephants.*

Right: *The symmetrical placement of the large-paned windows makes the facade of the Château de Thoiry look transparent.*

The viscount and viscountess's children, Colomba and Edmond, right, *stand in one of the doorways of the château's dining room, which is adjacent to the kitchen. The pink-hued, ocher-colored walls are an effective background for the family portraits. Many of the furnishings, including the elaborate serving dishes and the busts, have belonged to the castle for more than four hundred years.*

Left and below, left: *The original kitchen, although modernized, is as warm and informal as the rest of the château. Paintings of domestic animals—roosters, peacocks, and hares—double as doors to the pale wood cabinets.*

Right: *On the walls of the master bedroom is a very rare wallpaper that dates from the reign of Louis XVI. It was hand-painted in situ for the room by a Chinese artist who had been invited to the court. Family portraits are placed on the round table, which has been covered with a large embroidered shawl.*

MODERN ANGLES
IN AN OLD CASTLE

Located near Les Baux in Provence, this 18th-century château, with stone walls and rounded-tile roofs, was built in the architectural style typical of the region. The castle's profile is one that fits in well with the ruggedness of the countryside, as well as with its climate—hot and dry in the summer and exposed to the unrelenting wind of the south (known as the Mistral). Although the château—which is made up of a series of buildings and includes a round tower—looks relatively small on the outside, the interior offers a series of soaring, dramatic spaces, surprising in their modernity.

The present owners have lived in the château since 1950 and have not only renovated the building but furnished it in a style that combines the traditional handicrafts of the area and an angularity not unusual in modern French interior architecture.

Right and below: *The exterior of the mid-18th-century castle has been unchanged. The small windows and stone walls keep the interior cool. The red tiles used for the roofs of the different parts of the structure are typical of the southern region.*

Above: *An 18th-century Proven-çal commode, a modern Italian lamp by Richard Sapper, and a 19th-century romantic painting exemplify the mix of furnishing styles in the modernized interior.*

Above, right: *The large interior spaces of the castle are dramati-cally punctuated by a soaring semicircular arch and a long open second-floor pass-through.*

Right: *The dark pieces of furni-ture contrast with the walls, which are all white.*

Right: *The black wrought-iron dining room chairs are copied from 18th-century regional de-signs, and their striking silhou-ettes are played off against the curved architecture.*

Above: *In the mid-18th century the roomy fireplace was used to both heat the interior and cook the food for the castle.*

Left: *The large eat-in kitchen, which opens onto a courtyard, is as old as the castle itself but has been completely renovated. A long counter preparation area is topped with local tiles.*

Right: *The enormous ceiling-hung fireplace is a graphically strong element in the living room designed by an American architect, Peter Harnden.*

LOOKING INSIDE

Unlike the British, whose famous bow windows seem to invite glimpses into the home, the French tend more to shield themselves from the outside world. Shutters protect the house from sun and wind by day and secure it at night. But most windows are not without their decorative interest.

Grilles and cutouts, fences and window boxes, all contribute to the lively and decorative views along French streets. Whether in the small windows of the stone country houses or the more generously proportioned windows of urban residences, there is always something of interest to catch the eye.

Above and left: *Windows from the Parisian suburbs to the Pyrénées display a variety of architectural and ornamental styles.*

The term French window calls immediately to mind an elegant, classical aperture; two windows, actually, opening majestically into the room and equipped with shiny, elaborate hardware. The windows often overlook a balcony or open onto a terrace. Shutters on the exterior and a well-defined system of curtains and draperies on the interior were once de rigueur. Sheer or lace curtains allowed light to come in during the day, yet afforded a certain amount of privacy; drawing the thick double drapes was an evening ritual.

Left, top and below: *The lace patterns on curtains can be intricate or simple. A boldly handworked cluster of grapes is an unusual variation.*

Right: *In Monique Petit's Paris house, an extravagant lace curtain screens a view of the grotto.*

Left: *Interior designer Jacques Grange hung a voluminous, loose curtain of white cotton in front of a window, creating a nearly sculptural form.*

180

Right: *An unusual bowed window of small glass panes at the Château de Varengeville in Normandy, which was designed by the English architect Edwin Lutyens, is framed by two flowing white slivers of curtains.*

Left: *A double French window frames a spectacular view of Paris's Place des Vosges in Jean-Claude Binoche's apartment.*

Right: *Floor-to-ceiling opaque glass doors, which were original to the 1930s house, separate the front reception rooms in Agnès Comar's Art Deco interior.*

LIVING

Left: *A flared-arm chair from the 1930s and a bowl of carved wood fruit create a still life in Agnès Comar's living room.*

Right: *A gilt-edged, cream satin upholstered armchair is in the classical 18th-century Paris living room of Paloma Picasso and her husband, Rafael López-Sanchez.*

From the era of Louis XV until about 1960, there were few significant changes in the French living room. Called the "salon," it was the room where one received guests and important family questions were presented for serious discussion. Since it was not a place to relax, the furniture—chairs, primarily—was made for sitting upright, making polite conversation, and being on one's best behavior.

The room was always distinct from the adjoining dining room, from which one might adjourn for conversation after a meal. Television was one catalyst for changing the salon into a multipurpose room, as was the simultaneous discovery of the sofa—a more comfortable piece of furniture.

Recently, a taste for more old-fashioned furniture has, in part, prompted a return to formality, and the living room's ceremonial aspects are being appreciated once again.

The old-fashioned European salon or living room, full of amply proportioned sofas and chairs, has maintained its appeal. In many French apartments this room is used for formal receiving and as the center of family activity. So it is expected to be comfortable and yet elegant, up to date and yet not without a certain sense of nostalgia.

Right: *The high-ceilinged living room in the apartment of Clara Saint, a fashion publicist, faces the Seine River. Its peach-colored walls and upholstered seating contribute to the room's warm and feminine tone. A turn-of-the-century Turkish rug covers the parquet floors; an 18th-century painting leans on a stained oak console from the 1930s.*

The rigorous geometry of the interior spaces of Art Deco buildings of the 1930s and 1940s can elicit different design responses. Their spacious, often square high-ceilinged living rooms are most often appointed with furniture from the period, which gives them a formal air. But the same attention to structure and architecture can also act as an inspirational background for a more imaginative, younger approach, whereby shapes and colors are played off against one another with a decidedly sure French hand.

Left: *In furniture and fabric designer Agnès Comar's Paris house, the shapes of the reception rooms are based on the geometry of the circle and the square. The living room armchairs, reupholstered with velvet dress fabric, are from the 1930s. Crystal Lalique pigeons and boxes are displayed on an Art Deco table. Beyond, a gray marble table sits squarely on the graphic marble floor, which is original to the 1930s house.*

Right: *The primary colors and angular shapes of the four armchairs, reproductions of circa 1917 designs by Gerrit Rietveld, the Dutch De Stijl architect, are composed against the bright palette of an antique American patchwork quilt hung on the wall.*

The need to furnish an apartment on a limited budget, but without sacrificing a sense of style, is often the impetus for fresh, inventive design. It is a practical form of illusion and one at which the French are particularly adept. Currently in vogue is a subtle form of theatricality reminiscent of interior designer Jean-Michel Frank and tinged with a surrealism that brings to mind the work of playwright Jean Cocteau.

Far left: *Artist Mattia Bonetti's all natural-hued living room has an air of surrealism.*

Left and above: *The curtains and loose slipcovers were made from cotton sheeting. Bonetti's sculpture models are displayed on top of an appliquéd straw cabinet. The wrought-iron grille is from a shop window display.*

The high ceilings, the inlaid marble floors, and the gracious proportions of rooms in many French 18th-century buildings offer opportunities for designing on a grand scale. One could choose to restore these spaces to the way they looked in the past, but instead new occupants are using them as showcases for a fashionably cluttered and eclectic interior where a mix of colors, textures, fabrics, patterns, and periods—Venetian-type mosaics, neo-Egyptian and neo-Gothic objects—all coexist in the same time and place.

Far left: *In Paris, Kim and Odile Moltzer's living room looks more Italian than French.*

Above and left: *Angel Ponce de Leon has reproduced an Andrea Palladio drawing on one wall. The neo-Gothic stove came from a Paris antiques shop. The stone lioness is English.*

In France, as in England, one interpretation of modernism is an informal style based on the use of natural materials such as straw, cotton, and blond woods coupled with plain off-white walls and simple shapes. It is a comfortable style of decoration, with Scandinavian overtones. Traditional furniture pieces, sometimes ordinary, functional designs that are no longer in production, have been revived and used with more modern pieces.

Far left, above, and left: *In interior designer Michèle and Gilles Mahé's living room, a rocking deck chair and a wood folding table—usually terrace furniture—are paired with a large classic sofa. The painted canvas on the wall is by Gilles Mahé, an artist and journalist. The two hanging lamps and the overscale furnishings contribute to the room's strong graphic quality.*

The furniture designed in Austria at the beginning of this century is now in particular favor in the United States and France—especially the designs by Josef Hoffmann, one of the cofounders of the influential Wiener Werkstätte movement, whose pieces are seen as the inspiration of today's modern furniture styles. Collectors often look for the complete suites that were customary in that era's rooms. The settee, side chairs, and tables would match, and even a hat rack or lamp might be bought to complete the suite.

Above: *Eric Philippe, a Paris antiques dealer, and Léonore Bancilhon have furnished the large main space of what was once a ceramics studio with a number of suites of furniture, all from the early 20th century. Under a 1929 painting by Ecuadorian artist Manuel Rendon, Philippe has positioned a Viennese bentwood and pressed cardboard suite of furniture that dates from about 1910, by the architect Robert Oerley.*

Above: *Josef Hoffmann designed this bentwood settee, side chairs, and lounge chairs for J. J. Kohn in about 1905. The 1900 lamp is probably Italian; the view of Rome, a 1924 work by Jules Flandrin; the bronze box on the table that dates from about 1900 is by Georg Klimt.*

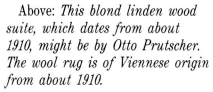

Above: *This blond linden wood
suite, which dates from about
1910, might be by Otto Prutscher.
The wool rug is of Viennese origin
from about 1910.*

Above: *Nineteen-thirties artist
and decorator Armand-Albert Ra-
teau hand-carved the frames of
these two solid oak lounge chairs,
which have been reupholstered in
satin moiré fabric.*

Contemporary French interiors have not escaped the reign of beige—that neutral, tasteful background against which paintings and sculpture can best be displayed. Blank walls, stripped of ornate moldings, are perfect foils for art, as are the more classical furniture designs. But although this approach may be seen as part of an international design style, it is one that has been adroitly refined in the French idiom.

Stacks of neatly piled up books and simple groupings of objects, as well as leather chairs and sofas, add a feeling of warmth to these uncluttered, "well-heeled" rooms. These are living rooms that are not only nice to look at but provide the necessary comforts to make the interior work—and in which every painting or piece of sculpture is esteemed a masterpiece whether it is or not.

Left: *The living room of Bernard and Laura Ruiz-Picasso's apartment with its pale yellow walls and honey-colored carpeting acts as a backdrop for part of the collection of works by his famous grandfather, the Spanish painter Pablo Picasso. A large oil simply stands on an easel; a custom-made black granite table holds a silver platter by Picasso, some small African sculptures, and a series of Danish porcelain ashtrays. The leather chairs and sofa are by Le Corbusier.*

Above: *On the other side of the room, a geometric painted screen is placed in front of the built-in bookcases. On the shelves is Bernard Ruiz-Picasso's collection of American, Japanese, and German robots dating from the late 1930s to the early 1960s.*

Left: *A number of works by Pablo Picasso are arranged on the mantelpiece, which has been painted by Gilles Massart to resemble lapis lazuli stone. Picasso made the little horse in front of the fireplace out of a television stand, in 1960, as a gift to his grandson.*

Right: *Jean-Charles and Catherine de Castelbajac's large apartment, in a turn-of-the-century Paris building, offers the couple a space in which to display their collection of modern art. Two large terra-cotta urns are from Vallauris, a village on the Côte d'Azur famous for its pottery. They flank a low gray marble table on which are set three pieces by Claudio Parmigiani, an Italian conceptual artist whose work also leans against the wall. An Aubusson-style rug is in the foreground.*

Above: *The painted door, glimpsed at left, was in the apartment when the fashion designer Jean-Charles de Castelbajac and his wife, Catherine, moved in, but its elaborately decorated surface was discovered only after it was cleaned. There is a Chinese carpet in front of the deep caramel-colored leather sofa, which is situated to leave part of the living room open and uncluttered. A kneeling stool is the only other piece of seating in this part of the room.*

Right: *A table faces the seating group around the fireplace. The large plants and the painting hung high over the old-fashioned mantel only hint at the room's high ceilings. Photographs and personal mementos are propped up against stacks of books.*

EATING

Among the well-to-do in late-19th-century France, the greatest compliment for a visitor was an invitation to share in the ritual of a traditional meal.

The meal was a formalized affair, taking place in a dining room that was commonly far from the kitchen and furnished with a sideboard on which the china and cutlery were carefully displayed. Chair rails on the walls and, in some cases, markers on the floor delineated where the chairs should be positioned after meals.

When shrinking residential spaces forced the living and dining functions of the house to be compressed into one room, it was not unusual to designate a "coin repas" as well as a "coin salon." But even when relegated to a small corner, the dining room held its own, and was often furnished with a large table and enough chairs to accommodate a large family.

Right: *Set off against a stripped pine floor are an oval dining table, bentwood chairs whose seats are engraved in an iris pattern, and a bowl of carved fruit.*

In France, the presentation of food is never taken lightly—the sheer visual pleasure of a meal before it is eaten is an essential part of dining. Fish platters and cake stands, dishes for asparagus and tarts, fluted vases, decorated pitchers, and crisp white table linen are the accessories for sublimely beautiful and appetizing repasts.

Left: *In the country kitchen at Château de Thoiry, a shelf of spices and preserves has been installed in front of a tromp l'oeil painting of a magnificent meal: fish in a basket, an assortment of fresh fruit, a sculptural cake, and a vintage bottle of wine.*

Right: *Pacha Bensimon's traditional marble-topped buffet came originally from a bakery. It is now used as a sideboard to hold silverware and dishes as well as a group of shapely pears and apples set on cake stands.*

Whether it's winter or summer, there's always something appealing about eating in a garden atmosphere. But in many French city apartments, where light is frequently at a premium, the illusion of being outdoors can be difficult to create. Walls painted with a garden scene, big bouquets of fresh flowers, and well-tended plants contribute decoratively to the feeling of dining alfresco, even if it's all happening indoors.

Left: *Antique outdoor metal chairs and a table—all painted white—are set up for eating in this veranda room, which is adjacent to a real garden. The serving buffet and the patterned floors are both made of stone.*

Below, left: *A wicker chair and a small square table are set up in a corner of Nadine and Etienne Roda-Gil's Paris apartment facing a large window as a quiet place to dine alone. The landscape on the wall is painted in trompe l'oeil.*

Right: *Vertical blinds are hung in front of the windows of Janine Roszé's dining room, which has a southern exposure. The bright room has been furnished with cane chairs and a white marble-topped oval table.*

Below, right: *Healthy plants flourish in this light-filled dining room with its long wood table and bistro-type chairs.*

One form of inspiration in European interior design has been the American Postmodern architectural movement of the last few years, which relies on such classical elements as columns, arches, and Etruscan, Greek, or Roman details. The result can be very sophisticated, as in this striking pink-and-black room, which features a series of floor-to-ceiling columns intriguingly reflected in the mirrors.

Above and right: *In Paris, Patrice Ellif conceived a neoclassical dining room for the Place des Vosges apartment of Jean-Claude Binoche, an art collector.*

Left: *Detail of the columns and the intentionally illusionistic way in which they are reflected.*

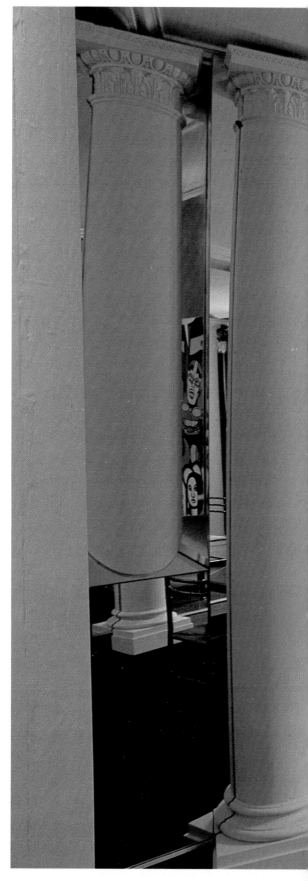

Re-creating the flavor of the past is a favorite decorating approach in France. Whether dining rooms are sophisticated or more ingenuous, their china, linens, and furniture seem to lend themselves especially to this kind of stage setting.

Above: *Jacqueline Dufour's unusual Paris dining room is focused around a large turn-of-the-century Renée Marval painting in muted colors of a reclining woman. It is a collector's room, where each object was chosen not only for its intrinsic value but for the way it works with the rest of* the furnishings. *A lamp from about 1900 is set on a late-19th-century antique brass table in front of a Jean Dunand screen painted with swallows. The wrought-iron table and chairs from the 1930s were found in an antiques shop.*

Above: *Nadine and Etienne Roda-Gil created a nostalgic and charmingly naive dining area in their apartment, part of a 1906 Parisian building. The color scheme of the room is kept mainly to white—the paneled walls, the antique lace tablecloth, the fabric and bead lamp from the 1920s. A built-in niche of shelves surrounds the simple trestle table and wicker chairs. The Roda-Gils were inspired by some early-20th-century floral motifs to paint the decorative friezes on the wall. The delicate patterns work well with the dainty yet functional pieces of china and basketry displayed on the shelves.*

The relationship between the shape of a dining room and the proportions of the table and chairs chosen for it is always a matter of much deliberation. Round rooms are rare, but when they exist their special geometric qualities should be taken advantage of to the fullest.

Left: *In the apartment dining room of fashion designer Jean-Charles de Castelbajac and his wife, Catherine, a round table echoes the unusual room, which has a window set in a rounded wall. The mouse gray walls and the small round-backed chairs contribute to the traditional feeling. The blue-and-yellow china made in Limoges is a reproduction of the dishes used by the impressionist painter Claude Monet in his house at Giverny.*

Below: *The other side of the room is squared off. A painting by conceptual artist Olivier Mosset leans against the wall.*

Right: *Agnès Comar, a home furnishings designer who specializes in pillows and fabrics, has a round cloth-covered dining table surrounded with a set of angular 1930s chairs that came from a department store tearoom. The dining area is partially open to the living room beyond.*

COOKING

The kitchen of a French home, in the country or in the city, has traditionally been a separate realm reigned over by the women of the household, whether mother, grandmother, or cook. It was a room in which children were allowed for certain meals, and then only if they behaved, and where some men dared not even tread.

The country kitchen was a central room and the place in which many activities of the house were carried out. The urban kitchen was often smaller, equipped with just the bare essentials.

The American kitchens of the 1950s, with work islands, cabinets, gadgets, and appliances, represented a financially unobtainable ideal of efficiency for many Europeans. Their apartments and houses did not come with built-in equipment or kitchen cabinets; for them, the furnishings for a kitchen more often represented a serious commitment.

There are two aesthetics that are reflected in the fully equipped modern French kitchen: the warm, cluttered country kitchen with its checkered floor, cast-iron stove, and open shelves of dishes and china, and the sleek, high-tech-inspired kitchen with exposed ductwork but in which all equipment is kept neatly out of sight behind trim, flush cabinet doors.

Left: A pale green and off-white selection of summer vegetables adorns a marble-topped table in the kitchen of a summer house.

Above: *In Kim and Odile Moltzer's Paris kitchen, a Provençal cloth covers a table at which all meals are taken. The checkered floor is traditional. A shiny stainless steel restaurant stove has been installed near an antique cast-iron unit, which still works.*

The eat-in, live-in kitchen, which has been the center of peasant and country houses for centuries, has in the last few decades taken on a new status. In the country, and even in the city, it is now considered fashionable to eat and entertain in the kitchen. And the elements found in traditional French kitchens—the checked tile floor, antique cast-iron stove, copper pots, and bleached pine furniture—once taken for granted, are now the keys to a cherished new aesthetic.

Right: *A knife rack is conveniently hung over a small table equipped with a cutting board surface. Some of the bread is trompe l'oeil ceramic.*

Below: *A small antique toy stove, which still functions, is displayed on top of the black cast-iron oven.*

In many of the older, classical apartment buildings, the kitchen was originally installed as far away from the dining and living areas as possible. It was a practical layout for its day, when people had servants, and both cooking noises and odors were thought best kept away from the rest of the house. But that layout is not convenient for today's more informal life-style. So when the opportunity to renovate these spaces arises, the architectural features of the kitchens are preserved, but they are sometimes moved into one of the apartment's more pleasant and usually brighter front rooms. They thus provide the all-purpose family and entertaining area that is becoming ever more popular in Europe, as in the United States.

Left: *Designer Denis Doria planned a modern and minimal black-and-white eat-in kitchen in what was once the dining room in an 18th-century building in the Saint-Germain-des-Prés section of Paris. The floor is covered in black rubber and both the compact and efficiently planned work island and the dining table are topped with black plastic laminate. A collection of Lalique glass vases is on top of the antique ceramic fireplace from Austria.*

Above: *Black Le Corbusier bentwood chairs are placed on either side of the dining table. In the middle is a Lalique glass centerpiece.*

When updating a kitchen, one often finds that an original element, an old-fashioned wood- or coal-burning stove, for instance, can provide an interesting focal point for the new design and an attractive contrast to the cooler aesthetic and efficient look of modern appliances. Kitchens in which wood is used, whether inspired by the country kitchens of the past or the modern kitchens of Scandinavia, are popular. The influence of the United States can be seen in the streamlined storage cabinets that are sometimes replacing freestanding pieces of furniture and in the use of modern appliances, such as wall ovens, cooktop ranges, and large refrigerators.

Left: *In Jacques and Sophie Seguela's turn-of-the-century house in Neuilly, near Paris, the original kitchen was completely modernized by Christian Duval of the architectural group SOPHA. The work island has a built-in sink. The delicacy of the pale rose marble tabletop is played off against the matte gray ceramic floor and wall tiles and the old-fashioned wooden kitchen chairs.*

Right: *Corinne Bricaire, a fashion designer, had a cast-iron table custom-made for her Paris kitchen. Stove and cooktop are incorporated into the table, over which hangs a large specially made hood. Bought at an auction, the large antique file cabinet with its roll-top desklike doors is used for storing china.*

Below, right: *Knotty pine is the main material of this kitchen in a vacation house in the Vendée. A large round white table on a pedestal base is surrounded by a set of black wrought-iron upholstered chairs. Both the refrigerator and the wine racks are built into the paneled wall.*

Left: *A round table with bentwood chairs is at the center of this old-fashioned kitchen. Lots of plants, the cream-colored walls, and the glass-doored wood cabinets add to its appeal.*

Below, left: *In a summer house in the country, a tiny kitchen has been installed. The deep double sink can accommodate large pots and pans; spoons and implements are kept on the windowsills.*

Right: *In the Château de Chazeron in Auvergne, in the center of France, is this very ancient and atmospheric kitchen in the Louis XIII style, dating from the 16th century. Glass bottles and pottery, some native to the region, are displayed above wood-burning ovens made from local volcanic stone.*

There is a strong tradition in France of treasuring the materials and equipment of daily life—simple functional utensils, well-worn copper cookware, shiny wood bowls, classically shaped pottery. While the aesthetic appeal of leaving these unpretentious objects out in view has only recently begun to be appreciated by Americans, it is an attitude that has been long honored in French kitchens.

Far left, above and below: *Enamel racks and containers, a wood basket, plain all-white china, and a rolling pin are both useful and decorative.*

Left: *Clear glass bowls and decanters, wineglasses and water glasses, are conveniently stored on a white shelf unit of a vacation house kitchen.*

Right: *A huge black cast-iron stove is both the functional and the visual focus of this high-ceilinged Paris kitchen.*

The white country kitchen, appointed in bleached wood, has become a French classic. Easy-to-clean tile floors, uncluttered countertops, and open shelves are often features of these kitchens.

Above: *A cupboard, which once held papers and supplies in a notary's office, is used for dishes in this fresh-looking kitchen on the Ile de Ré across from the town of La Rochelle on the Atlantic coast of France. The oak shelves on the wall were made by a village craftsman, the marble tabletop is an antique.*

Above and left: *A blue marlin hangs over the doorway of this summer-house kitchen with painted stone walls, also on the Ile de Ré. The house was originally a barn. The white ceramic-tiled counters are edged in oak; the table is covered with a piece of black oilcloth, a convenient surface for cleaning fish.*

Sleek modern kitchens, which have their origins in the American efficiency kitchens of the 1950s, are far from commonplace in France. But the high-tech kitchen, with commercial fixtures and hardware, restaurant appliances, stainless steel counters, and exposed ducts, has grown in popularity, as has eating and inviting guests into a room that was previously out of bounds.

Right: *In the Paris kitchen of Yvon Lambert, designer Andrée Putman has given the industrial look a sophisticated, understated, and elegant point of view. All the usual kitchen paraphernalia, along with china and accessories, is stored out of sight in cabinets with doors covered in small gray ceramic tiles. The thin strip of red tiles, set into the white tiled walls, is meant to recall the border of traditional French kitchen towels. The duct above the work surface draws out cooking odors.*

SLEEPING & BATHING

In considering French bedrooms one can't help but recall the ceremonies that surrounded the awakening and retiring of Louis XIV, the "Roi Soleil." It was a high honor then for courtiers to be invited to the levér or the coucher of the king. The "chambre à coucher" could also be the "boudoir," the woman's sanctum, which, translated literally, was the place "to sulk."

Bedrooms were not only for sleeping, but places to retreat, dine, and think, and gen-erally prepare oneself to face the outside world. Many French writers and artists have favored that room over all others. Marcel Proust was known to receive visi-tors while in bed; Colette wrote surrounded by cats in her bed overlooking the gardens of Paris's Palais Royal.

In poorer homes, entire families often slept in the same room. In many country houses, a canopy bed, in the main living space, gave the only privacy and warmth.

Far left and left: *A painted and lacquered bed from the 1880s, with a lace-edged pillow and embroidered bedcover, and an antique piano furnish one of the children's bedrooms in Monique Petit's suburban Paris house.*

One expression of contemporary French design is the slick, expensively appointed interior, which could approach the garish were it not tempered by a sure, sophisticated hand. This style is particularly suited to bedrooms. Furnished with luxurious materials—satins, leathers, and deep pile wool carpeting—they are sensuous environments and an ideal backdrop for personal collections of art.

Left: *A curious pyramidal staircase by interior designer Patrice Ellif leads ceremoniously to the upstairs floor of Jean-Claude Binoche's Paris duplex apartment. On the walls is a complete suite of engravings by one artist.*

Below, left, and right: *The master bedroom is furnished with a desk by Jules Leleu, an Art Deco cabinetmaker and designer, and a bed, graceful side chair, and slim, red-lacquered cabinet by Eugène Prinz. The paintings are by modern French and Italian artists.*

Today the installation of a bathtub or sink in the bedroom is often space-saving, but it recalls the old-fashioned French bed-and-bathrooms in which the sink was often hidden behind a screen. In contemporary bedrooms the bath or sink, if integrated, is left visible and designed so as to coordinate with the rest of the space.

Creating an attractive sleeping and bathing environment is often possible even with limited means. A room may be focused around a window view, or designed to complement a particular collection. The unusual geometric patterns and bright colors of Early American patchwork quilts are favored in many French bedrooms.

Top, left and right: *Jacques and Sophie Seguela had a combination bed-and-bathroom built over a garage in a Paris suburb; the bath, right, is at the top of the steps, hidden behind the bed.*

Above, left: *A guest bedroom designed by Jacques Grange has an integral step-up bathroom. The tub and sink are enclosed in stained pine. The countertops are granite. The muted colors are set off by crisp white linen.*

Above: *The sparse, clean look of this bedroom, with its painted stone walls, shiny wood floors, and unmatched furniture, suits its location in a vacation house.*

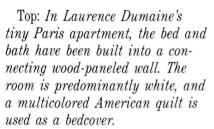

Top: *In Laurence Dumaine's tiny Paris apartment, the bed and bath have been built into a connecting wood-paneled wall. The room is predominantly white, and a multicolored American quilt is used as a bedcover.*

Above: *In a simply furnished country bedroom, a small step-stool serves as a bedside table and a piece of fabric hangs on the wall in lieu of a headboard.*

Top: *American folk art—duck decoys, baskets, and samplers on the wall, as well as a red-and-white patchwork quilt—contribute to the country-style look of René Legrand's bedroom.*

Above: *This bedroom overlooks Paris's Jardin de l'Observatoire and is furnished on a garden theme. There is a trellis on one wall, a green-and-white quilt on the bed, and a wicker chair in front of the open window.*

There are few countries where the sense of personal taste is as developed as in France, or where unique and totally individual designs are carried off with such élan.

Foreign influences—from Egypt, Japan, Africa, or Greece—have always been welcomed and easily integrated. But it is the exotic rather than the merely foreign that is the most seductive.

Above, left and right: *Interior decorator Jacques Grange created a neo-Egyptian bedroom out of a theater set by customizing the theater flats to fit the walls of a Parisian bedroom and making a four-poster bed out of the columns. The neo-Gothic lamp over the bed fits in with the decor, as do the striped carpeting, which was copied from a late-19th-century design, and the side table, made of faux bamboo ceramic. The bedcover is cashmere, and the hieroglyphics-patterned sheets are from an American department store.*

Left: *The bathroom walls are newly painted deep peach, but the stained-glass window belonged to the theater set. The bathtub and sink were originally in an old Parisian hotel.*

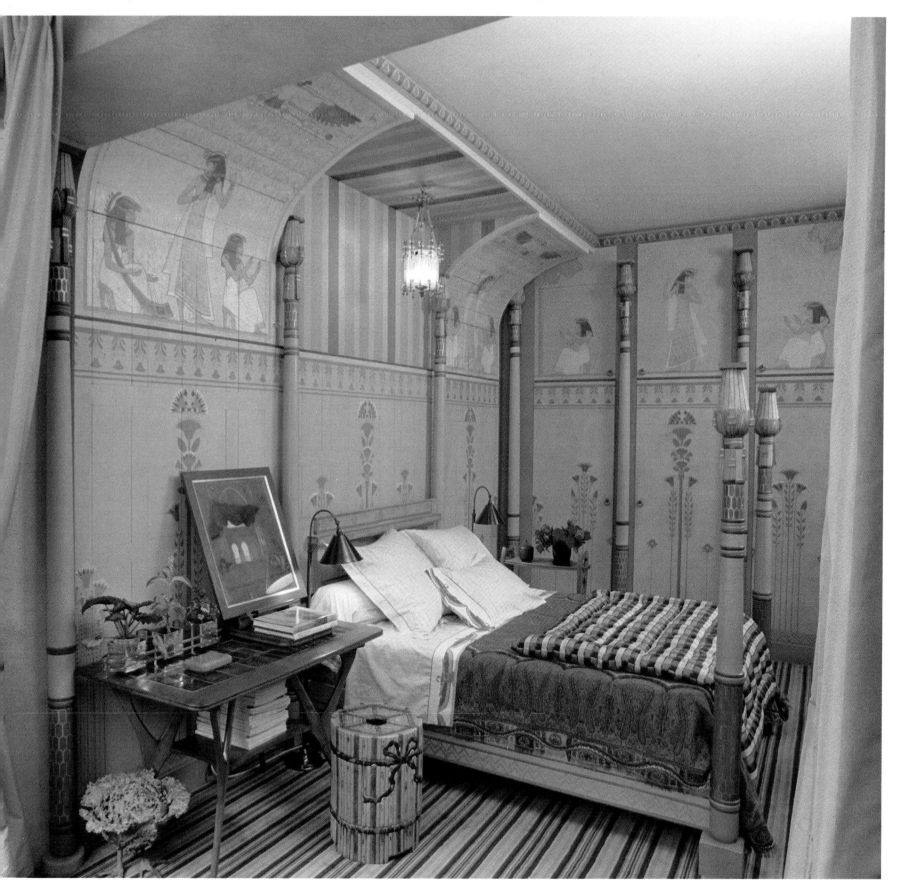

Courtesy Maison de Marie Claire, Hirsch-Mariel Dirand

Because many old French houses do not have adequate bathrooms, the renovations of these structures offer opportunities to plan such rooms from scratch. Instead of installing simply utilitarian fixtures, people are taking these rooms one step further. Bathrooms tend to be larger and more luxurious—rooms meant for pleasant relaxation.

Top: *Separated from the bedroom by only a series of white lacquered doors, this summer-house bathroom has an urbane look. The bathtub is freestanding, the sink an antique from an old hotel. Towels and supplies are kept in a pine corner cabinet.*

Above: *An effort was made to integrate this small bathroom into the rustic style of the country house in which it was newly installed. The stuccoed walls have been worked in a swirling pattern.*

Top: *In the Saint-Tropez house of fashion designer Daniel Hechter, Oriental shoji-type wood screens are used for the shower enclosure and cabinet doors.*

Above: *The centrally placed footed tub with its remarkable brass fixtures is the focal point of interior decorator Alberto Pinto's bathroom in a Paris hotel particulier. The oil painting stretched on the wall, the wood floors, and the Victorian easy chair contribute to the salonlike feeling.*

Right: *Madison Cox's small white-walled bathroom is clean and simple. The sink on legs is similar to ones seen in many European hotels. The hardware is a reproduction of antique nickel-plated fixtures.*

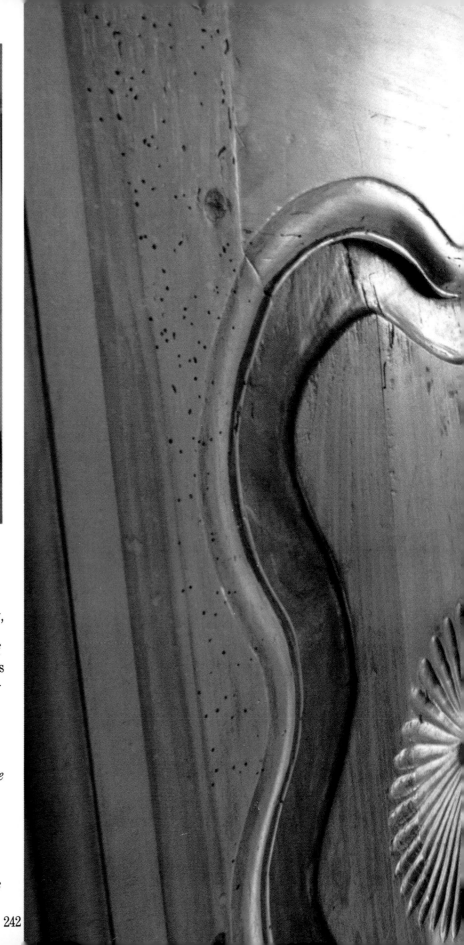

Bedrooms are private rooms, where fashion often gives way to comfort and where furnishings are selected as aids to relaxation. Opening a bedroom door, if only halfway, can offer glimpses of a world that is entirely separate from the rest of the house. In France, even bedrooms in strikingly modern homes are usually traditional in design, with bedside tables and reading lights, lots of soft pillows, and opaque curtains for the windows.

Above: *Rough, textured walls are an appropriate backdrop for this country bedroom corner.*

Right: *The soft light, square-paned windows, fine fabrics, and delicately patterned carpet contribute to the Gallic charm of this old-fashioned room.*

Above: *Near the bed are a group of shiny globes and striking black-framed photographs.*

Right: *The paintings of pillows by Miguel-Ange Yrazazabal are played off against the real pillows in these two adjacent Parisian bedrooms. The choice of primary colors is unusual, as is the way more modern design elements—the bed set at an angle, the over-the-bed table and white walls—update fashion designer Popy Moreni's classically proportioned high-ceilinged apartment.*

Above: *The small religious images on the wall and the objects on the cloth-covered night table evoke a sense of innocent country charm. The antique oil lamp, an oval mirror, the blue-circled cup and saucer, a bouquet of just-picked field flowers, and delicate stems of lavender tied into a ribbon spindle are all part of a timeless still life.*

Right: *The antique pitcher and cup set in a niche in the stone wall of this country house convey the tone of this wood-beamed bedroom. The metal bed frame is painted pale yellow; the bedcover is traditional white cotton.*

Not only changing tastes but the vicissitudes of the intervening decades have made it rare in Europe to come across interiors of quality that were designed in the 1930s and 1940s and have survived intact.

This is especially true in the case of kitchens or bathrooms, rooms that have always been subject to modernization. Even in France, where many of the best designers and architects of the period created interiors when a new bathtub or sink was affordable, not much consideration was given to the aesthetic value of the existing fixtures.

Left: *When Jean-Luc Buyo, a photographer, answered an advertisement for a Paris apartment "in need of renovation," he was surprised to find this absolutely remarkable bathroom by Jules Leleu, the cabinetmaker and designer who was responsible for the interior decoration of many ocean liners of the period. Buyo didn't touch a thing. The bathroom, with its organically shaped sink made of red-and-gold mosaic tile, was designed by Leleu about 1932. The bathroom is entered after walking down a flight of steps, as if one were descending into a swimming pool. The walls are made of ceramic elements that imitate the bamboo in relief; the floor and steps are of red, yellow, and black ceramic tile.*

Above, right: *The primary-colored lounge chair, a reproduction of a Gerrit Rietveld design, was chosen to parallel the rhythmic color scheme of the mosaic tile.*

Right: *A large window opens onto the Bois de Boulogne. Storage is hidden behind a wall of pivoting mirrored panels against which a series of tube-shaped light fixtures have been installed.*

249

Fabric and lots of it has always been a trademark of French interiors. In the more sumptuous bedrooms, walls were upholstered, curtains and draperies were generously flounced, and bed linens were finished with elaborate lace.

But the number of craftsmen capable of doing this kind of quality work has diminished, and there are now fewer people able to afford such expensive decorating touches. So young designers have come up with alternatives—cotton sheeting replaces silks and damasks; walls are painted instead of lacquered to evoke a sense of luxury with more modest means and a lighter touch.

Left: *François Baudot, a decorator and a consultant to The Palace, a Paris discothèque, designed a canopied tent structure for his bedroom using white cotton sheets. The always freshly laundered linens convey a bright summerlike feeling all year round. Only typically French plants that are usually seen outdoors—geraniums and ivy—are included in the indoor setting. The only color deemed pure enough by the designer to offset the white fabric was a clear red for the surface behind the bed. A white plaster bust lies under a wrought-iron chair.*

Left: *Marie-Hélène Massé, a Paris publicist, wanted to create a world suitable for a courtesan in her tiny apartment. The late-19th-century bed with a scalloped footboard and headboard of etched mirror, the blood-red walls, and the mirrored wall sconces fitted with red candles contribute to the intensely feminine room that is not without its sense of fun.*

COLLECTING

Left: *In Gordes, in southern France, two pottery vases sit on the corner of a carved mantel.*

Right: *Michèle and Gilles Mahé's mantelpiece holds a striking collection of objects of different shapes and textures. The black-and-white fireplace contrasts with the pattern of the African textile; the smooth surfaces and gentle curves of the bowls and vases, with the rough texture of the bunches of natural grasses.*

In France, collecting is not so much a hobby as a way of life. People never tire of exploring the marchés aux puces—the flea markets—the antiques shops, or their grandmothers' attics. Although there are serious collectors of objets d'art, many people seem to have an eye for the unusual and are attracted to shape and color in the things they like, no matter what the value. French collectors have a true sense of discovery and can transform the plainest pieces of pottery and glass, the most common knickknacks, into engaging works of art simply by the way they display them in their homes.

In many French rooms, the fireplace and mantel offer an opportunity for the display of originality and a talent for mixing a variety of objects of different sizes, shapes, textures, and colors. The mantel, and the wall above it, can become the strong visual focus of the room.

Left: *The cubistic painting and the row of small sculptures and mineral samples create a series of busy patterns set against the paneling of the room.*

Below, left: *An off-center composition of personal mementos is dominated by the wood-framed picture of a small boy.*

Bottom, left: *The squareness of this plain white mantel is contrasted with the rhythmic succession of the circular plates and the softness of the dried flowers.*

Right: *In Dany Simon's Paris house the fireplace has been covered in white ceramic tile. A modern Italian lamp by Richard Sapper, a mirrored sphere, an antique brass lamp, and a fishbowl vase full of fresh flowers have been selected for their rounded shapes.*

Below: *The mantel of a black-and-white tiled fireplace is used to display a collection of flea-market finds in this Paris atelier.*

In most interiors, objects will always remain accessories. But in some especially inspired spaces the essence of the design is in the choice of objects and the way in which they have been positioned by a collector. Purposely grouped and displayed, they suggest an unexpected and curious mystery.

Far left: *In an illustrator's Paris apartment, a Venetian mirror hangs over the fireplace, which is painted white to match the rest of the space.*

Left: *The 1930s table in the dining room, with its stained oak top and wrought-iron base, is by Gilbert Poillerat.*

Below, far left: *The apartment is located under the eaves of an office building. Once a series of rooms, the spaces are now angular and have exposed metal beams and posts. The blue velvet upholstered sofa with its swan-shaped frame came from one of the duke of Windsor's houses.*

Left: *"Noah's Ark," a large painting by Leon Underwood dated 1919, hangs over a 1930s oak console. Displayed on the console are a man's head in wood by sculptor Ossip Zadkine, a Lachenal vase, and a bronze Japanese box.*

Right: *A column by interior decorator Jean-Michel Frank and two wrought-iron chairs from the 1940s are audaciously placed in front of the bookshelves.*

Left: *A book by Cecil Beaton, an anonymous German photograph, and a neoclassic gray-and-red painter chair create one of the apartment's intriguing still lifes.*

Right: *On the wall are four 18th-century portraits of Chinese men; on the side table, two 19th-century Chinese mannequin heads and a Japanese mask.*

Below: *In the studio a cabinet holds small crafts objects. To its left is an antique garden chair.*

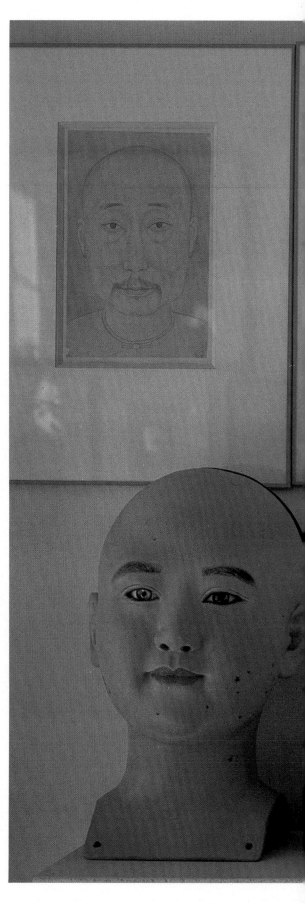

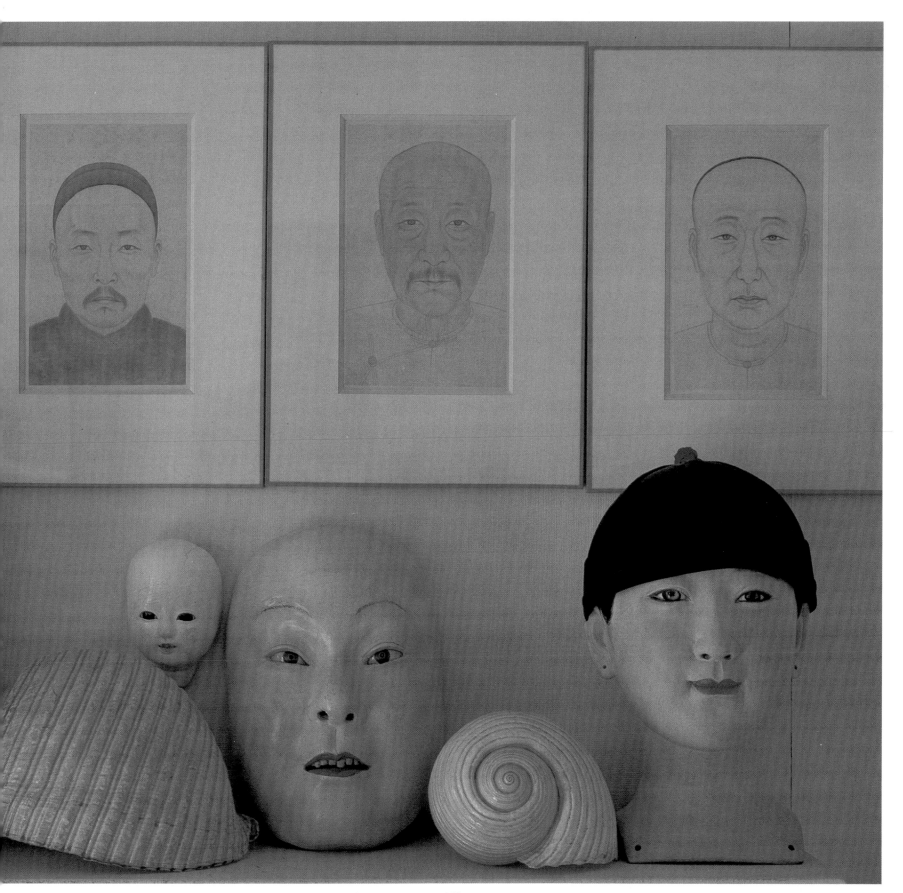

Some collectors develop a passion for one kind of artifact and even before they realize it find their homes not unpleasantly overtaken by the ever-increasing number of objects of affection. But it is rare to find an unusual collection in a house that is itself a collector's item.

But architect George Candilis, once a student of Le Corbusier, happened upon an extraordinary structure in Paris's Montparnasse area, an 1840 building that had once accommodated a photography studio. In 1850 the building had been purchased by an artist, who added two floors. The addition was inspired by a Thai temple and was in keeping with the current fashion for Orientalism.

Left, below, and bottom: *The exterior of the house, a combination of carved beams and pilasters as well as a patchwork of ceramic tiles, was known for its use of Oregon pine, never before seen in Paris. It seems fitting that the extraordinary wood structure should now hold Candilis's collection of Thonet bentwood furniture.*

Right and below: *The curved backs of two pieces of furniture exemplify the fluidity and gracefulness of bentwood. Michael Thonet had developed a way of molding plywood for chairs in 1830 and by the 1850s had perfected the process using steam to bend solid wood.*

Bottom: *Rocking chairs, like this one, first appeared in Europe right after the middle of the 19th century.*

Once mass-produced, original bentwood is now rare and prized by collectors. Candilis's collection is exceptional because of the quality and number of pieces he has managed to assemble under one roof.

Above: *The dining room is completely, even traditionally, furnished with bentwood. The small settees, dining chairs, and tables are all part of the collection.*

Above: *The living room is a bentwood bonan-
za—lounge chairs and rockers are lined up next
to one another. A chair is hung on the wall,
and a small child's chair or salesman's sample
is displayed in the middle of the table.*

Disparate knickknacks old and new, precious and mundane, high style or kitsch, are enticing to collectors even of modest means.

Left and below: *The shelves in the house of the artist known as Ben are used to display a very eccentric collection of objects that include advertising memorabilia, a gumball machine, pitchers, a stuffed bird, and Art Deco figurines.*

Above: *A mustachioed gentleman from the turn of the century portrayed on glass, wood hat forms and pottery pitchers, a specialist's assemblage of antique seals and boxes, and a gardenlike display of flowers in small glass vases offer different views of collecting.*

As in many European countries, there is a long tradition of basket weaving in France. Of all shapes and sizes and for sundry purposes, baskets are not only decorative objects to collect but can prove useful household containers.

René Legrand lives near Paris, on the banks of the Marne River, in a house that was once a small local restaurant. The owner of the Quatre Saisons home furnishings shops, Legrand has in the last few years ferreted out, all across France, the traditionally crafted things he particularly likes.

That only begins to explain the collection of baskets piled high on a garden cart, left, and practically bursting from the storage house in his garden, below left and right.

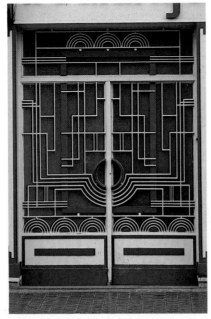

LOOKING OUTSIDE

Far left and left: *A series of country and city doors and doorways and a stone archway at the Château of Varengeville in Normandy are intriguing sights.*

Doorways in French cities are usually protective barriers between private courtyards and busy streets; in the country, doorways often lead from village paths to the seclusion of a beautiful garden. Over the centuries, edged in stone, carved in wood, engraved with decorative numbers, the doors and doorways of France have been one of the country's most stylish elements.

French terraces and gardens, with perfectly clipped hedges and organized parterres, are often the direct if modest descendants of the formal gardens at Versailles. Other times they champion the controlled exuberance of such gardens as painter Claude Monet's at Giverny.

Some vegetable gardens are carefully cultivated like rose gardens; some terraces rely more on stones and bricks than plants for their design. French gardens are most of all civilized, a gentle transition between the outdoors and the indoors.

Left: *A cluster of old china pitchers and bowls are left outside on a table on the terrace of this French Riviera house.*

Below, left: *Bowls and plates made by local craftsmen and cutlery used for eating out of doors are left to dry on a garden table in the Roussillon region.*

Right: *The spacious terrace that is situated at the back of artist César's Mediterranean villa has a floor of inlaid marble, and a large umbrella of unbleached linen to provide shade. The chairs surrounding the table—some cast-iron, some rattan—are deliberately mismatched.*

Above: *The geometrically clipped topiary shrubs, the low, colorful flower beds, and the well-defined stonework are part of the formal approach to this small-scaled, traditional French garden.*

Above: *Interior decorator Dick Dumas takes a relaxed approach in his south of France garden. Terra-cotta pots hold plants and flowers on a tiered stand, and luxuriant greenery climbs the stone walls.*

Above: *A long metal table and metal-backed chairs furnish this sheltered terrace garden.*

Above: *There is a profusion of plants in the shaded terrace of interior decorator Dick Dumas's house in the south of France. In the background: a large zinc star. In the foreground: old café chairs and a tabletop made from an old church clockface.*

Above: *An antique wood column stands in an archway—its texture offset by the stone walls of this old garden in the south of France.*

Above: *A birdcage and a collection of kitchen gadgets form a still life on a stone wall under one of the small windows of this converted barn in the Roussillon.*

Left: *An antique wire bottle rack is used to carry a variety of glasses from house to garden.*

DOSSIER

In this dossier, we have provided importers and retailers of French antique and contemporary furniture, bed and table linens, carpets, fabrics and wall coverings, lighting, cookware and tableware, hardware and tiles. Department stores such as Harrods, Liberty, Heals and John Lewis are the best sources for a wide range of French merchandise. Antique shops are numerous nationwide. Camden Passage and Westbourne Grove in London, for instance, are worth exploring. In the case of such famous names as Baccarat crystal, Le Creuset cookware and Roche & Bobois furniture, importers can provide retail information in your area. We have also included products that are popular in France, though not French in origin, such as chairs by Charles Rennie Mackintosh, Rietveld and Charles Eames, Laura Ashley fabrics or English bathrooms. Although we have tried to include as many diversified sources as possible, the dossier is meant to be used as a guide rather than a definitive listing. Every effort has been made to be accurate; but if some sources have not been included and some addresses have changed, we will endeavour to correct future editions.

Photographs by Robert Levin

ANTIQUE FURNITURE

AND SO TO BED
638 Kings Road, London SW6
Tel. 731 3593
Branches in Halifax, Bolton,
Tyne & Wear
*More reproductions than antique
beds, mainly in brass*

ARCHITECTURAL ANTIQUES
Ainsleys Ind. Estate, Elland,
West Yorks HX5 9JP
Tel. 0422 78125
*All kinds of elements rescued from
demolition sites*

BLANCHARDS
178 Sloane Street, London SW1
Tel. 235 6612
*European and Far Eastern
furniture*

Rococo mirror

BUNZL & DAVAR
344 Kings Road, London SW3
Tel. 352 3697
*Mainly Continental 17th- and
18th-century provincial furniture*

CIANCIMINO LTD
104 Mount Street, London W1
Tel. 499 2672
*Oriental and Far Eastern
furniture*

COBRA
149 Sloane Street, London SW1
Tel. 730 2823
*20th-century 'antique' styles, Art
Deco, etc. Furniture, lamps,
objects*

COLEFAX & FOWLER
39 Brook Street, London W1
Tel. 493 2231
*Antique and painted furniture that
can also be made on order*

CONRAN SHOP
77 Fulham Road, London SW3
Tel. 589 7401
Some country furniture and objects

CSAKY'S ANTIQUES
20 Pimlico Road, London SW1
Tel. 730 2068
*17th-century English and
Continental furniture*
133 Putney Bridge Road,
London SW15
Tel. 870 1525
Pine furniture, doors, fireplaces

DREAMS
34 Chalk Farm, London NW1
Tel. 267 8194
Brass beds and patchwork quilts

ELIZABETH EATON
25a Basil Street, London SW3
Tel. 589 0118
Antique furniture and objects

GLOUCESTER HOUSE ANTIQUES
Market Place, Fairford,
Gloucestershire
Tel. 0285 712790
*English and mainly Continental
provincial furniture*

GREAT BRAMPTON HOUSE ANTIQUES
Madley, Hereford
Tel. 0981 250244
*Pre-1830 English and Continental
furniture*

HALTON FOUR POSTER BEDS
3 Cadogan Street, London SW3
Tel. 589 1860
Antique and reproduction

JONES & RAYNER
24 Baddow Road, Chelmsford,
Essex
Tel. 0245 57639
*Reproduction of French period
furniture*

NETHERBROOK ANTIQUES
86 Christchurch Road, Ringwood,
Hants
Tel. 04254 2062
*English and Continental country
furniture, decorative objects*

TETBURY ANTIQUES
39a Long Street, Tetbury,
Gloucestershire
Tel. 0666 52748
Mainly French furniture

DAVID TREMAYNE LTD
320 Kings Road, London SW3
Tel. 352 1194
Lacquer and Far Eastern furniture

Eighteenth-century armoire

O. F. WILSON ANTIQUES
Queen's Elm Parade, Old Church
Street, London SW3
Tel. 352 9554
English and Continental furniture

Art Deco furnishings

CONTEMPORARY FURNITURE

ARAM DESIGNS
3 Kean Street, London WC2
Tel. 240 3933
Eileen Gray, Rosenthal, Shiro Kuramata, Marcel Breuer, Le Corbusier and their own designs

JAMES ARCHIBALD & SONS LTD
6-14 Great Western Road, Aberdeen, Scotland
Tel. 0224 56181
Italian and French furniture

BAKER, KNAPP & TUBBS LTD
26 King Street, London WC2
Tel. 379 6366 (showroom)
American furniture, reproduction and modern. Will provide lists of retailers

BLANCHARDS
178 Sloane Street, London SW1
Tel. 235 6612
American, Italian and French furniture and objects

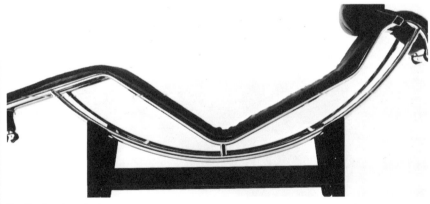
Le Corbusier chaise

CIANCIMINO LTD
307 Kings Road, London SW3
Tel. 352 2016
Own designs

CLASS INTERNATIONAL
31 Sloane Street, London SW1
Tel. 235 8452 (showroom)
Will provide list of retailers

CONRAN SHOP
77 Fulham Road, London SW3
Tel. 589 7401
Italian chairs, Continental and English shelves and furniture

DOMANI FURNITURE
23 Newman Street, London W1
Tel. 580 3371 (showroom)
Cardin designs

Thonet bentwood chair

ENVIRONMENT
179 Shaftesbury Avenue, London WC2
Tel. 240 5057 (showroom)
Distributors for Cassina furniture. Will provide list of retailers

GENERAL TRADING CO.
144 Sloane Street, London SW1
Tel. 730 0411
Mainly Italian furniture

DAVID HICKS LTD
101 Jermyn Street, London SW1
Tel. 930 1991
Own designs

Art Deco chair

HOPEWELLS
Huntingdon Street, Nottingham
Tel. 0602 57611
Italian, French, German, Scandinavian and American furniture

MAPLES
26 Bond Street, London W5
Tel. 579 9134
52 High Street, London SW19
Tel. 946 6531
141 Tottenham Court Road, London W1
Tel. 387 7000
Great mixture of international modern and of reproductions

MASKREYS
116 Witchurch Road, Cardiff
Tel. 0222 29371
Commercial Road, Newport, Gwent
Tel. 0633 67061
62-66 White Ladies Road, Pliston, Bristol
Tel. 0272 738401
French and Continental furniture, objects

CHARLES PAGE
61 Fairfax Road, London NW6
Tel. 328 9851
French furniture: Roset, Maugrion, Mahé, Breuer. American: Charles Eames

H. PONSFORD LTD
London Road, Sheffield
Tel. 0742 550075
Italian furniture: Vandel, Turri, Szediv

ROCHE & BOBOIS
50 Baker Street, London W1
Tel. 486 1614
Continental furniture, objects

Rietveld chair

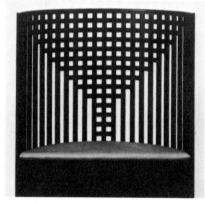
Mackintosh 'Willow' chair

ROSET LTD
95a High Street, Great Missenden, Bucks
Will give addresses of retailers for this French firm

TOWNHOUSE INTERIORS
25g Lowndes Street, London SW1
Tel. 235 3189
Italian furniture

Herbst chair

OSCAR WOLLENS
421 Finchley Road, London NW3
Tel. 435 0101
*Italian, Scandinavian, German,
French furniture: Rietveld, Le
Corbusier, Marcel Breuer and also
Mackintosh*

ZARACH
48 South Audley Street,
London W1
Tel. 491 2706
*Lacquered furniture. Swiss,
Italian and French: Mahé,
Charpentier*

CARPETS

AFIA
81 Baker Street, London W1
Tel. 935 0414
*Modern and designers' carpets,
mainly wall to wall*

DAVID BLACK
96 Portland Road, London W11
Tel. 727 2566
*Oriental rugs and most origins,
antique*

BLANCHARDS
178 Sloane Street, London SW1
Tel. 235 6612
Modern carpets

FAIRMAN CARPETS
218 Westbourne Grove,
London W11
Tel. 229 2262
*Antique Oriental and Far Eastern
rugs*

C. JOHN
70 South Audley Street,
London W1
Tel. 493 5288
*Oriental, Indian and French
antique carpets*

VIGO CARPETS GALLERY
6a Vigo Street, London W1
Tel. 439 6971
*Oriental and Continental antique
carpets*

FABRICS AND WALLCOVERINGS

JAMES ARCHIBALD & SONS LTD
6-14 Great Western Road,
Aberdeen, Scotland
Tel. 0224 56181
Fabrics in stock

LAURA ASHLEY
183 Sloane Street, London SW3
Tel. 235 9728
35 Bow Street, London WC2
Tel. 240 1997
*Wallpapers and furnishing fabrics.
Has a catalogue for sale in
newsagents, listing all branches
nationwide*

BLANCHARDS
178 Sloane Street, London SW1
Tel. 235 6612
*Papers and fabrics, English and
Continental*

COLE & SONS
18 Mortimer Street, London W1
Tel. 580 2288
*Large choice of English and
Continental wallpapers; Zuber
panoramic hand-printed papers*

COLEFAX & FOWLER
39 Brook Street, London W1
Tel. 493 2231
*English and Continental fabrics,
wallpapers, trimmings and carpets*

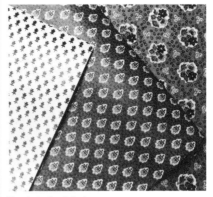
Souleiado fabrics

CONRAN SHOP
77 Fulham Road, London SW3
Tel. 589 7401
*Own designs in upholstery and
curtain fabrics; Indian fabrics and
rugs*

ELIZABETH EATON
25a Basil Street, London SW3
Tel. 589 0118
*English and Continental fabrics
and wallpapers. Will supply
names of retailers as well*

DAVID HICKS
101 Jermyn Street, London SW1
Tel. 930 1991
*Own designs in fabrics and
wallpapers*

LINDSAY HISCOX
Edith Grove, London SW10
Tel. 352 9377
*English, American and French
wallpapers and fabrics: Pierre
Frey, Manuel Canovas, etc.*

HOME DECORATING
83 Walton Street, London SW3
Tel. 584 6111
*English and Continental
wallpapers and fabrics. Objects*

INTERIOR SELECTION
240 Blythe Road, London W14
Tel. 602 6616
*English and Continental
wallpapers, fabrics and carpets*

JONES & RAYNER
24 Baddow Road, Chelmsford,
Essex
Tel. 0245 57639
*Continental and English fabrics
and wallpapers*

JOHN OLIVER
33 Pembridge Road, London W8
Tel. 727 3757
*Wallpapers, English and
Continental. Own range of paints*

OSBORNE & LITTLE
304 Kings Road, London SW3
Tel. 352 1456
*Own designs in wall coverings and
fabrics. Retail nationwide.*

Glazed cotton fabric

PALLU & LAKE
18 Newman Street, London W1
Tel. 636 0615
*French wallpapers: Jean Vigne,
Nobilis. Fabrics from Casal,
Chanee, Ducrocq, and trimmings*

PAPER MOON
12-13 Kingwell, 58-62 Heath
Street, London NW3
Tel. 431 3035
*Wall coverings from Sweden,
France, Canada and Italy*

PEACOCK
3 White Hart Lane, London SW13
Tel. 878 3012
Wall coverings and fabrics from international catalogues

PENNICK & OWERS
23-27 The Pantiles, Tunbridge Wells, Kent
Tel. 0892 35051
International selection of wall coverings, fabrics and carpets

A. H. PERCHERON LTD
44 Berners Street, London W1
Tel. 580 1192 (showroom)
Importer and distributor of French wall coverings

SANDERSON
53 Berners Street, London W1
Tel. 636 7800
Very large range of English and international wall coverings and fabrics, including William Morris. Own range of paints

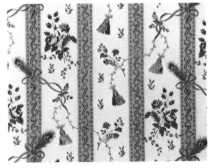

Glazed cotton fabric

SCARISBRICK & BATE LTD
111 Mount Street, London W1
Tel. 499 2043
Italian, French wall coverings

SOULEIADO
171 Fulham Road, London SW3
Tel. 589 6180
Provençal wallpapers, fabrics and plastified fabrics of traditional exclusive design

TISSUNIQUE LTD
10 Princes Street, London W1
Tel. 491 3386 (showroom)
Importer of exclusive French fabrics: Frey, Prelle, Canovas. Silk and gold brocade from Louis XIV's bedroom at Versailles. Will supply list of retailers nationwide

Upholstery fabric

TOWN HOUSE & COUNTRY HOUSE
458-62 Crow Road, Glasgow
Tel. 041 3572250
English and Continental wall coverings and fabrics

TURNER WALL COVERINGS
32 Grosvenor Street, London W1
Tel. 491 7056 (showroom)
68-78 Brewery Road, London N7
Tel. 609 4909
Imported wall coverings of all kinds

WATTS & CO
7, Tufton Street, London SW1
Tel. 222 7169
Woven fabrics, stamped velvets and trimmings

ARAM DESIGNS
3 Kean Street, London WC2
Tel. 240 3933
Contemporary Italian designs: Flos, Arteluci, etc.

ATRIUM
POB 6, Harpenden, Herts
Importers of contemporary Continental light fittings

BAKER, KNAPP & TUBBS LTD
26 King Street, London WC2
Tel. 379 6366 (showroom)
American designs. Will supply list of retailers

MR LIGHT
275 Fulham Road, London SW10
Tel. 352 7525
Contemporary Continental and English light fittings

TOWNHOUSE INTERIORS
25g Lowndes Street, London SW1
Tel. 235 3189
Italian designs

CHRISTOPHER WRAY LIGHTING EMPORIUM
600 Kings Road, London SW6
Tel. 736 8434
Any kind of style, antique reproduction and modern. Large choice

ZARACH
48 South Audley Street, London W1
Tel. 491 2706
Painted wooden lamps

BONNET LTD
10 Bromley Road, Beckenham, Kent
Will supply list of retailers

R. BOSCH LTD
POB 166, Watford, Herts
Will supply list of retailers

GAGGENAU
Colville Road, London W3
Tel. 993 2332 (showroom)
Will supply list of retailers

GOLDREIF KITCHENS
226 Tolworth Rise South, Surbiton, Surrey
Tel. 337 0082
Will supply list of retailers

LEICHT KITCHENS
Lagoon Road, Orpington, Kent
Will supply list of retailers

MOBALPA
Unit E, Griffin Ind. Estate, Stephenson Road, Toffon, Southampton
Will supply list of retailers

POGGENPOHL LTD
226 Tolworth Rise South, Surbiton, Surrey
Will supply list of retailers

PROWODA LTD
Headbrock, Kington, Herefordshire
Tel. 0544 230789
Will supply list of retailers

SIEMATIC
11-17 Fowler Road, Hainault Ind. Estate, Ilford, Essex
Will supply list of retailers

ZENKO KITCHENS
Manor House, Barby Lane, Barby, Warwickshire
Tel. 0203 79969
Will supply list of retailers

Pepper mill

COOKWARE AND TABLEWARE

ASPREYS
165 New Bond Street, London W1
Tel. 493 6767
Baccarat crystal, Limoges porcelain, Christofle silverware, Lalique glass, porcelain and glass ornaments

BONDS
9 All Saints Green, Norwich, Norfolk
Tel. 0603 60021
Cookware and tableware, English and Continental

Copper double boiler

CLARBAT LTD
302 Barrington Road, London SW9
Tel. 274 4771
Importers of enamel and cast-iron utensils: Le Creuset, etc.

CONRAN SHOP
77 Fulham Road, London SW3
Tel. 589 7401
English and Continental cookware and tableware, mostly French

BARBARA COURTENAY
21 St Osmund's Road, Parkstone, Poole, Dorset
Tel. 0202 734549
Importer of copperware

COURTIER & CO. LTD
400 Durnsford Road, London SW19
Tel. 946 8891
Importer of enamelled cookware

RICHARD DARE
93 Regents Park Road, London NW1
Tel. 722 9428
English and Continental cookware and tableware

Melior coffee pot

DARTINGTON GLASS LTD
4 Portland Road, London W11
Tel. 727 6472 (showroom)
Dartington glass. Will supply list of retailers

ELIZABETH DAVID
46 Bourne Street, London SW1
Tel. 730 3123
Cookware and tableware, English and Continental. Distributes nationwide as well

DIVERTIMENTI
68 Marylebone Lane, London W1
Tel. 935 0689
Mostly Continental and French kitchen utensils and crockery

THE FRENCH KITCHEN
86 Westbourne Grove, London W2
Tel. 229 5530
Cookware and tableware of professional standards

GENERAL TRADING CO.
144 Sloane Street, London SW1
Tel. 730 0411
English and Continental china, glasses and kitchen utensils

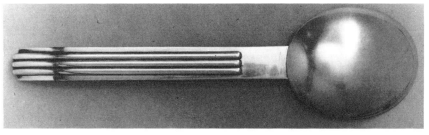

Puiforcat Beauville Silverware

'Monet' china

GRAHAM & GREENE
7 Elgin Crescent, London W11
Tel. 727 4594
An assortment of cookware and tableware from various countries

HABITAT
156 Tottenham Court Road, London W1
Tel. 387 9021
Many branches in London and nationwide. Catalogue for sale in newsagents
Cookware and tableware of English and Continental origin

ICTC LTD
632-652 London Road, Isleworth, Middlesex
Tel. 847 2411 (showroom)
Importers of French cookware and tableware: Cie Nat. de Porcelaine; Luneville porcelain; tin, copper and stainless steel pans, etc.

LEON JAEGGI & SONS LTD
232 Tottenham Court Road, London W1
Tel. 580 4038
Mainly cookware for the trade

DAVID MELLOR
4 Sloane Square, London SW1
Tel. 730 4259
English and Continental cookware and tableware

Quimper plate

'Basket' china

ROMANI
Watergate Street, Chester,
Cheshire
Tel. 0244 27719
*Mainly French tableware and
cookware*

LINEN

ANNA'S CHOICE
Belford Mills, Riverside,
Kilmarnock, KA1 3JP
Tel. 0563 20115
*Mail order lace curtains and
bedspreads. Will send catalogues
and samples*

CONRAN SHOP
77 Fulham Road, London SW3
Tel. 589 7401
*Bed linen, mostly French; table
linen from France, India, and
China*

Primrose Bordier pillowcase

DESCAMPS
197 Sloane Street, London SW1
Tel. 235 6957
*Own exclusive designs. Also
distributed nationwide*

FRETTE
98 New Bond Street, London W1
Tel. 629 5517
Italian designs

Gingham napkins and dish towels

HABITAT
156 Tottenham Court Road,
London W1
Tel. 387 9021
Many branches in London and
nationwide. Catalogue for sale in
newsagents
*French and Indian bed and table
linen*

LUNN ANTIQUES
86 New Kings Road, London SW6
Tel. 736 4638
Antique lace

Le Jacquard Français linens

Antique lace tablecloth

HARDWARE

BERNARD ARMELL & CO LTD
17-21 Sunbeam Road,
London NW10
Tel. 965 6094
Continental baths and fittings

BONDS
9 All Saints Green, Norwich,
Norfolk
Tel. 0603 60021
*English and Continental
bathrooms*

MRS BURGOYNE
33 Arthur Court, London W2
Tel. 229 5534
*Importer of French bathroom
fittings and decorations:
Porcelaine de Paris*

CRISTAL & BRONZE LTD
60 Queenstown Road, London SW8
Tel. 622 4191
*Importer of Continental
accessories for bathrooms*

CZECH & SPEAKE
39 Jermyn Street, London SW1
Tel. 439 0216
*Edwardian range of bathroom
fittings and accessories and one
model of Edwardian bath. All
reproductions in brass or gold
plated*

DAMIXA LTD
10 Woodcock Road, Ind. Estate,
Warminster, Wilts
Tel. 0985 214683
Modern taps

EWINGS
98 Cheetham Hill Road,
Manchester
Tel. 061 8322309
Modern baths and fittings

ORIGINAL BATHROOMS
143 Kew Road, Richmond, Surrey
Tel. 940 7554
*English baths of different shapes;
English, Italian and French
fittings and accessories*

HUMPHERSONS & CO. LTD
Beaufort House, Holman Road,
London SW11
Tel. 228 8811 (showroom)
Modern bathrooms and kitchens

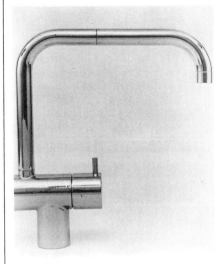

Vola fixture

MAX PIKE
4 Eccleston Street, London SW1
Tel. 730 7216
*Italian massage bath; French
baths, fittings and accessories:
Jacob Delafont, Porcher, M.
Herbeau, J.-C. Delepine, MPJ tin
basins*

EDV PROWODA LTD
Headbrook, Kington,
Herefordshire
Tel. 0544 230789
*Importer of Continental bath
fittings and accessories:
Emailleries du Vendomois, etc.*

SITTING PRETTY
131 Dawes Road, London SW6
Tel. 381 0049
*English original and reproduction
period bathrooms*

B. & P. WYNN & CO.
Crosshold House, 18 Boston
Parade, Boston Road, London W7
Tel. 567 8758
*Wholesale. Exclusive bathroom
accessories, washbasins, etc. from
France: handmade by F. Vauthier,
Gerard Boizot. Taps from Julia*

Bath scale

GARDEN FURNITURE

GOSFILLEX
10 Chandos Road, London NW10
Tel. 965 2268 (showroom)
*Will provide list of retailers. Have
plastic modern and period
reproduction garden furniture*

W. W. HALL LTD
Elgar Road, Reading
Tel. 0734 875353
*Importer of French wooden garden
furniture*

KING FASTON LTD
The Green, Station Road,
Winchmore Hill, London N21
Tel. 886 8783
*Importer of garden furniture from
the Continent, and accessories*

TRICONFORT
Oak Street, Norwich, Norfolk
Tel. 0603 25287
*Importer of own range of garden
furniture. Will supply list of
retailers*

TROPIC GARDEN FURNITURE
31 Winchester Street, Basingstoke,
Hants
Tel. 0256 54745
*Importer of own range of garden
furniture*

TILES

A. Y. TILES
8 Sentinel Square, Brent Street,
London NW4
Tel. 202 5262
*Exclusive French and Italian tiles.
Distribute the Faiencerie de Gien*

CERAMIQUE INTERNATIONALE
386 Kings Road, London SW3
Tel. 351 3467
1 Royds Lane, Wortley Ring Road,
Leeds
Tel. 0532 795031
*Large choice of tiles from several
countries*

CORNWISE
168 Old Brompton Road,
London SW5
Tel. 373 6890
*Italian, French, German and
English tiles, some handmade*

ELIZABETH EATON
25a Basil Street, London SW3
Tel. 589 0118
Continental and English tiles

ELON
8 Clarendon Cross, London W11
Tel. 727 0884
*Clay tiles, glazed and unglazed,
mainly handmade, from Mexico,
France, Belgium and Holland*

HABITAT
156 Tottenham Court Road,
London W1
Tel. 387 9021
Many branches in London and
nationwide, catalogue for sale in
newsagents
*Few patterned designs and plain
coloured tiles*

LANGLEY LONDON LTD
The Tile Centre, 165 Borough High
Street, London SE1
Tel. 407 4444
*Importers of German, Swedish and
French tiles: Villeroy and Boch*

MAX PIKE
4 Eccleston Street, London SW1
Tel. 730 7216
Handmade French tiles

TILE MART
151 Great Portland Street,
London W1
Tel. 580 3814
107 Pimlico Road, London SW1
Tel. 730 7278
*Large range of English and
Continental tiles*

INDEX